TWO CEMETERIES FROM BRISTOL'S NORTHERN SUBURBS

edited by Martin Watts

A LATER IRON AGE CEMETERY AND ROMAN SETTLEMENT AT HENBURY SCHOOL, BRISTOL: EXCAVATIONS IN 2004

by Derek Evans, Neil Holbrook and E.R. McSloy

A POST-ROMAN CEMETERY AT HEWLETT PACKARD, FILTON, SOUTH GLOUCESTERSHIRE: EXCAVATIONS IN 2005

by Kate Cullen, Neil Holbrook, Martin Watts,
Anwen Caffell and Malin Holst

COTSWOLD ARCHAEOLOGY

Bristol and Gloucestershire Archaeological Report No. 4

By agreement with Cotswold Archaeology this report is distributed free
to members of the Bristol and Gloucestershire Archaeological Society
To accompany Volume 124 of the Society's *Transactions* for 2006

Cotswold Archaeology Bristol and Gloucestershire Archaeological Report No. 4

Published by Cotswold Archaeology

© Authors and Cotswold Archaeological Trust Ltd, 2006

Building 11, Kemble Enterprise Park, Cirencester, Gloucestershire GL7 6BQ

ISSN 1479-2389
ISBN 978-0-9553534-0-6

Cotswold Archaeology BAGAR series

1.   **A Romano-British and Medieval Settlement Site at Stoke Road, Bishop's Cleeve, Gloucestershire**, by Dawn Enright and Martin Watts, 2002

2.   **Later Prehistoric and Romano-British Burial and Settlement at Hucclecote, Gloucestershire**, by Alan Thomas, Neil Holbrook and Clifford Bateman, 2003

3.   **Twenty-Five Years of Archaeology in Gloucestershire: a review of new discoveries and new thinking in Gloucestershire, South Gloucestershire and Bristol, 1979–2004**, edited by Neil Holbrook and John Juřica, 2006

4.   **Two Cemeteries from Bristol's Northern Suburbs**, edited by Martin Watts, 2006

Series Editor: Martin Watts

Produced by Past Historic, Kings Stanley, Gloucestershire, GL10 3HW

Printed in Great Britain by Henry Ling Limited, Dorchester, DT1 1HD

FOREWORD

Dealing with the dead is a complex and emotive issue. Our awareness of death, and how we treat our dead, is central to our humanity, and respect for the mortal remains of the dead is an underlying principle of modern society. Yet the current pace of development in Britain regularly results in the exhumation of human remains, and it is usually archaeologists who are responsible for their excavation, storage and ultimate redeposition. To help us establish and maintain common and appropriate standards of respect and decency, publications such as *Guidance for best practice for treatment of human remains from Christian burial grounds in England* (English Heritage/The Church of England 2005) have been produced, and the profession's approach to this issue is underpinned by *The Vermillion Accord on Human Remains*, adopted by the World Archaeological Congress in 1989.

As well as respecting the remains of the dead, and the wishes of the dead and their relatives/community, the *Accord* also establishes respect for the scientific research value of human remains as a core tenet. In this publication, the fourth in our *Bristol and Gloucestershire Archaeological Report* series, we present the results of two cemetery excavations, and in the spirit of the *Accord* we hope to have balanced appropriate respect for the human remains reported on with the informational value that they hold. Even poorly preserved burials are capable of generating large quantities of data, so for the purposes of formal publication *the human bone* sections of both reports are in summary form only. To enable wider accessibility to data otherwise held in archives, full reports will be available on demand from Cotswold Archaeology (info@cotswoldarch.org.uk) for those who require more detailed information.

Despite their difference in date, the cemeteries at Henbury and Filton have some common attributes. Both feature a predominant (although differing) burial attitude and grave orientation, and neither were rich in grave goods. The juxtaposition of some graves and the (rare) intercutting of others at both cemeteries may well reflect family associations. That such attributes also relate to modern burial grounds reminds us of the very human nature of this type of archaeological resource. It is not just the informational value of human remains that makes their study so rewarding but also their associative value, which enables us to identify more closely with and better understand our forebears, both in life and in death.

Martin Watts
Head of Publications, Cotswold Archaeology
December 2006

CONTENTS

ABSTRACTS

A Later Iron Age Cemetery and Roman Settlement at Henbury School, Bristol

Excavations in 2004 at Henbury School, Bristol, revealed the truncated remains of 21 inhumation burials, making a total of 28 burials recorded at the site since 1982. Of these, 24 burials formed a dispersed cemetery of crouched inhumations, the vast majority of which were aligned north/south and lay on their left sides, with equal numbers of males and females (where sex could be determined) and only one child. Poor bone survival rendered radiocarbon dating invalid, and the cemetery is dated by only one grave good: a finger ring from the mid to late Iron Age. However, the cemetery clearly pre-dated a later rectangular enclosure of very late Iron Age (early 1st-century AD) date. Crouched inhumations from the later Iron Age are known from the region but are usually from pits or scattered, so the presence of this cemetery at Henbury is significant. Inhumation cemeteries of this date are rare in Western Britain, although they may have been quite widespread. Despite the dearth of surviving features within the subsequent enclosure, the scale of the ditches suggests it was a farmstead, and environmental evidence hints at both livestock rearing and cereal cultivation. Subsequent Roman activity was clearly intensive, and included a further four burials; although difficult to interpret it adds to a substantial amount of evidence for Roman activity to the north-west of Bristol.

A Post-Roman Cemetery at Hewlett Packard, Filton, South Gloucestershire

Excavations in 2005 at Hewlett Packard, Filton, revealed the truncated remains of 51 inhumation burials within an isolated post-Roman cemetery. All of the burials were extended and east-west aligned, and were arranged in rows and groups. The tradition of east/west-aligned graves is a common late Roman and post-Roman practice, and these were not necessarily Christian. The largest group comprised 24 burials clustered around a central grave that contained an unusual skeleton and evidence for a distinctive burial rite. Overall there were slightly more females than males (where sex could be determined) and ten children. Adult stature could only be calculated in a few cases; males were generally taller that the early medieval average, females shorter. No grave goods were recovered, but four radiocarbon dates obtained from human bone suggest a period of use sometime between the 5th and 7th centuries AD. There was no evidence for contemporary settlement within the immediate vicinity. Other post-Roman cemeteries that are culturally distinct from Anglo-Saxon influenced burials are known from the region. The absence of Anglo-Saxon cemeteries in South Gloucestershire suggests this area remained under British control in the 5th and 6th centuries. The abandonment of this cemetery may have been the result of changes in the religious landscape once the area finally came under Saxon control in the late 7th century.

A LATER IRON AGE CEMETERY AND ROMAN SETTLEMENT AT HENBURY SCHOOL, BRISTOL: EXCAVATIONS IN 2004

by Derek Evans, Neil Holbrook and E.R. McSloy

with contributions by
Wendy Carruthers, Sam Inder, Teresa Gilmore, Fiona Roe and Sylvia Warman

INTRODUCTION
by Derek Evans and Neil Holbrook

In 2004 Cotswold Archaeology (CA) carried out an archaeological excavation within the grounds of Henbury Secondary School, Marissal Road, Bristol, on behalf of HBG Construction Western Limited and Bristol City Council, Children and Young People's Services. The project was designed to mitigate the archaeological effects of the construction of a new school, leisure centre and associated works.

Henbury School lies on the north-west fringe of the city of Bristol, approximately 6km from the city centre (centred on NGR: ST 562 791; Fig. 1), on an area of flattish terrain at *c.* 39m AOD. The underlying geology of the area is mapped as Keuper Marl of the Triassic Period (BGS 1971). The natural substrate exposed during the excavation comprised reddish clay and grey limestone bedrock. Some 750m to the south of the school lies the Iron Age hillfort of Blaise Castle, which sits at one end of a prominent limestone ridge that runs south-westwards towards King's Weston. Less than 1km to the west of the school the land drops steeply onto reclaimed mudflats of the Avonmouth Levels.

The excavation area lay within a former playing field to the south of the school. Levelling operations to create the playing field in 1982 had led to the discovery of six burials of possible Roman date by members of the Bristol and Avon Archaeological Research Group (BAARG) (Russell 1983). These burials lay close to a possible alignment of the Roman road from Gloucester to Sea Mills (Margary 1973, 140–1, route 541). The route of the road is not known with certainty hereabouts. Russell and Williams (1984, 26) suggest that its line might be represented by a disused track ('Old Lane') once known as 'Old Gloucester Road' (Seyer 1821, 71–2) which was visible as a slight holloway crossing the playing fields (Fig. 2).

In 2001 plans were devised for the construction of a new school, and as part of the design process a staged programme of archaeological assessment and evaluation was undertaken. Following preliminary desk-based assessment (BaRAS 2001; Smith 2003) a geophysical survey was undertaken in 2002 (GeoQuest Associates 2002). This identified a number of linear, rectilinear and circular anomalies including two parallel ditches close to the area where the burials had been discovered. Twenty-one evaluation trenches were subsequently excavated across the playing fields by CA in 2003 (CA 2003; 2004). This demonstrated that while some of the geophysical anomalies had a comparatively recent origin the two parallel ditches dated to the Late Iron Age or Early Roman period. A

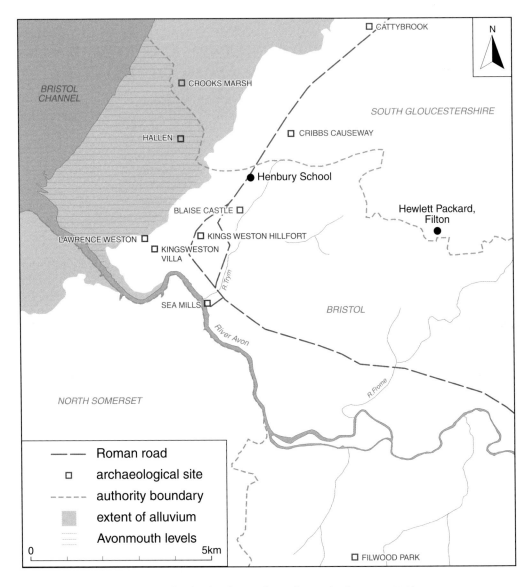

Fig. 1: Site location plan, with other local sites of significance (scale 1:100,000)

number of other features not detected by geophysics in the south-eastern part of the site dated either to this period or to the 3rd or 4th centuries AD. A single further inhumation burial was found. Two trenches (Fig. 2, trenches 10 and 11) were excavated across the putative line of the Roman road. These revealed a 3m-wide holloway which had eroded to a depth of up to 0.3m below the surrounding natural ground surface. The base of the holloway contained a rough stone surface which yielded post-medieval and modern finds. No trace of any Roman surface was found, and it is conceivable that any such deposits, if once present, have long since been eroded away. A stone-spread, associated ditches and a stone-built drain 125m to the south-east of 'Old Lane' was initially interpreted as the Roman road (Fitzpatrick 2004, 305) but subsequent excavation showed this to be part of a later Roman building. Medieval or later plough furrows and post-medieval or modern field boundaries and drainage features occurred throughout the site.

Planning permission was granted for the school development with a condition requiring advance archaeological excavation. A new sports hall was to be constructed in the south-east corner of the playing fields, the area of maximum archaeological potential defined by the evaluation. Accordingly the area to be disturbed by the hall (Area A) was excavated in March and April 2004. Subsequently it became apparent that further areas to the west of Area A would be disturbed by the construction of a water attenuation pond (Areas B and C). These were excavated in October and November 2004. In total an area of *c.* 1 ha was examined.

Fieldwork methodology

Fieldwork commenced with the removal of topsoil, subsoil and any areas of redeposited material resulting from landscaping by mechanical excavator equipped with a toothless grading bucket, under archaeological supervision. The archaeological features thus exposed were hand-excavated. Normally this involved the excavation of a 50% sample of discrete features such as pits and postholes, and up to a 10% sample of linear features. Where human remains were encountered, these were fully excavated in accordance with the requisite Home Office licence, and in some cases the fills of the graves were retained for off-site processing. All of the larger linear features were sampled in several locations, resulting in numerous context numbers being allocated to each feature. For ease of description these features have been allocated generic numbers. Artefactual dating evidence was recovered from the majority of excavated features. In many cases this dating is quite broad and features could only be assigned to general chronological periods. Within these periods, stratigraphic relationships between features allowed a more precise sequence to be established. Where features were uncovered from which no dating evidence was obtained, these have been assigned to particular phases based on their morphological character, location, stratigraphic relationship or proximity to other dated features.

Post-excavation methodology

Following completion of the fieldwork an assessment was made of the findings and a strategy proposed for further analysis (CA 2005). The assessment concluded that the period 1 (Later Iron Age/Early Roman) burials and settlement had good research potential to further our understanding of this period in the Bristol area. Consequently the artefacts and ecofacts associated with this period would be studied in some detail. The structural remains from the later Roman periods are less easy to interpret owing to the fact that they were only partly revealed at the extremities of the excavation area. Ground levelling in the central part of Area A also appears to have largely removed features relating to this period hindering an understanding of their plan and function. While it is considered important to present the structural evidence for these periods, the problems of interpretation and phasing suggested that further detailed analysis of the artefacts and ecofacts beyond that presented in the post-excavation assessment was not warranted. Within this report, capitalised features have been assigned a generic number; non-capitalised features retain their original context number.

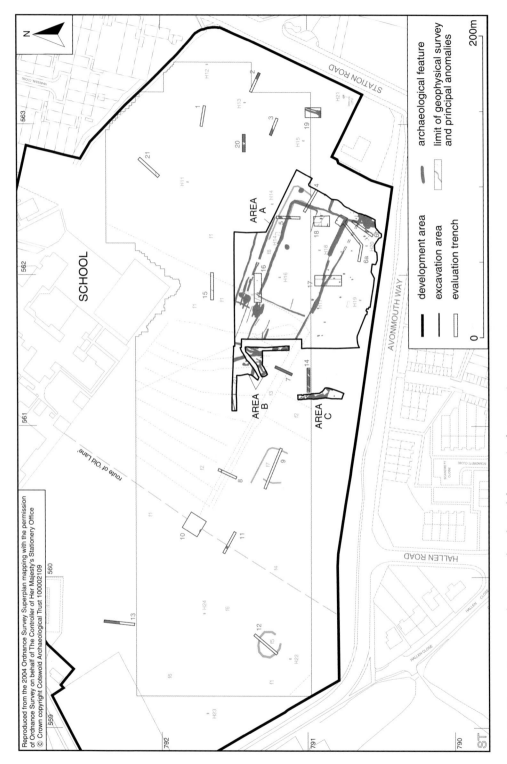

Fig. 2: Excavation areas, showing archaeological features (scale 1:2500)

EXCAVATION RESULTS
by Derek Evans

Archaeological deposits were encountered across each excavation area (Fig. 2). These had been heavily truncated, especially in the central part of Area A, during the construction of the football pitches in 1982. The features uncovered included a number of Middle or Late Iron Age inhumation burials, a sequence of Roman rectilinear enclosures, and a series of Late Roman limestone spreads which may have acted as bases for timber structures. The excavated features have been separated into the following chronological periods, with distinct phases of activity in each:

Period 1: Mid-Late Iron Age to Early Roman (4th century BC to 1st century AD)
Period 2: Roman (2nd to early 3rd centuries AD)
Period 3: Late Roman (later 3rd to 4th centuries AD)
Period 4: Post-medieval and modern

Period 1: Mid-Late Iron Age to Early Roman (4th century BC to 1st century AD)
(Fig. 3)

Phase 1
The remains of 24 single inhumation burials were uncovered within a zone c. 65m long and 25m wide adjacent to the south-eastern corner of Area A (Figs 3–4). This figure includes five of the burials uncovered in 1982 (R1, R3–6; Russell 1983) and the burial recorded in CA evaluation trench 17 (E1712; CA 2004). Details of the burials are contained in Table 1. Where sex could be determined the Period 1 population comprised seven males (including three possible examples) and five females (including three possible examples). All of the burials were of adults except SK14, which was that of a 9 to 10-year-old child. There was no clear pattern to the distribution of the burials within this space. The graves had fairly irregular, rounded cuts infilled with reddish brown silty clay, and varied in width from 0.45m to 0.93m and in length from 0.8m to 1.7m. The bones were in a moderate to poor state of preservation and were generally heavily truncated by later features and landscaping; in some instances graves only survived to a depth of 50mm; only one grave was deeper than 0.2m. Given the degree of truncation it is likely that further contemporary inhumations once existed at the site and have been destroyed.

In six instances (R4, R5, E1712, SK2, SK3 and SK12) these burials were so truncated as to render their layout within the grave unclear, but where the positioning of the skeletons could be determined they were all found to be crouched. Seventeen of the less-truncated burials were orientated roughly north/south, with the heads to the north (see Fig. 5 for typical example SK4); the exceptions were R1, R3, SK5, SK7, SK11 and SK13, which lay with their heads to the south (see Fig. 5 for SK5). Skeletons SK1, SK5 and SK9 were laid on their right sides, the rest of the skeletons were laid on their left sides. There was no obvious spatial patterning to these characteristics. There was no evidence for coffins and the majority of the skeletons fitted fairly tightly within their grave cuts.

There were two instances of intercutting graves (SK3 was cut by SK2 and SK20 was cut by SK19; Fig. 6), but all of these burials are considered to be broadly contemporary on the basis of their similar crouched postures, grave-cuts and backfills. The only grave good

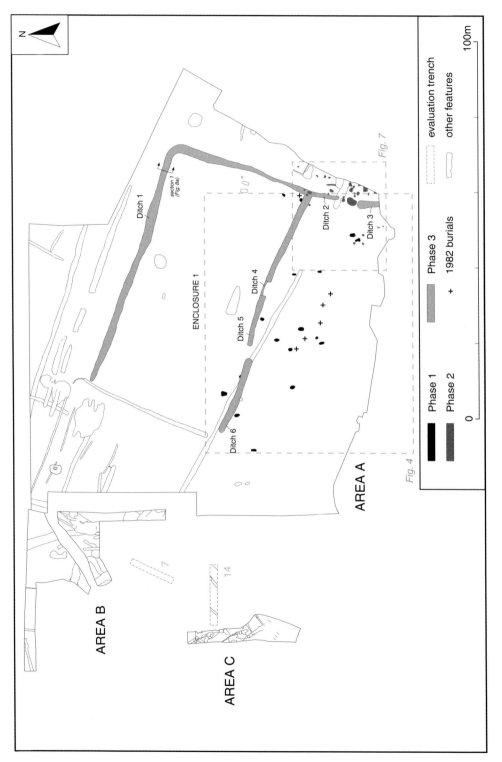

Fig. 3: Period 1, all features (scale 1:1000)

Table 1: *Summary of all graves, skeletons and dating evidence*

Pathology: CO: *cribra orbitalia*; DJD: degenerative joint disease; OA: osteoarthritis.

PERIOD	Skeleton	Grave depth	Preservation	Completeness	Age at death	Sex	Orientation	Body position	Pathology/condition	Notes/dating evidence
1	1	0.10m	moderate	40-45%	18+	m	N/S	crouched, on R		cuts SK3
1	2	0.07m	moderate	20-25%	26-35	m	N/S	-		cut by SK2
1	3	0.07m	moderate	5-10%	26-35	f?	N/S	-		
1	4	0.18m	moderate	40-50%	18-25	m	N/S	crouched, on L	periostisis of ribs and leg	
1	5	0.20m	moderate	80-90%	18-20	f	S/N	crouched, on R		stones placed over grave?
1	7	0.05m	moderate	15-20%	18+	u	S/N	crouched, on L		
1	9	0.30m	poor	20-25%	18+	u	N/S	crouched?, on R		Mid/Late Iron Age finger ring
1	11	0.07m	moderate	15-20%	18+	u	S/N?	crouched?		
1	12	0.05m	moderate	5-10%	18+	u	-	-		
1	13	0.10m	poor	10-15%	18+	u	S/N	crouched, on L		
1	14	0.07m	moderate	70-75%	9-10	-	N/S	crouched, on L		
1	15	0.10m	moderate	85-90%	26-35	f	N/S	crouched, on L		
1	16	0.05m	moderate	40-50%	26-35+	m?	N/S	crouched, on L		Radiocarbon date (pot residue): 930–800 cal. BC
1	17	0.14m	poor	70-75%	26-35	f?	N/S	crouched, on L	CO. trepanation?	
1	18	0.10m	poor	5-10%	26-35	u	N/S	crouched, on L		
1	19	0.20m	moderate	50-60%	36-45	m	N/S	crouched, on L	OA. DJD. Exostosis on finger	cuts SK20
1	20	0.13m	poor	15-20%	18+	f?	N/S	crouched, on L		cut by SK19
1	21	0.06m	moderate	0-10%	18+	u	N/S	crouched?		
1	E1712	-	poor	0-10%	18+	u	N/S	-		arm fragments only
1	R1	-	moderate	75-80%	18-25	u	S/N	crouched, on L		
1	R3	-	poor	10-15%	36-45	m?	S/N	crouched, on L		
1	R4	-	poor	not excavated	-	-	N/S	-		
1	R5	-	poor	0-5%	18+	u	N/S	-		
1	R6	-	poor	40-50%	26-35	m?	N/S	crouched, on L		
3	6	-	moderate	45-50%	18+	m?	N/S	extended, supine	broken ribs	neonate bone/animal teeth by skull. 16 Fe coffin nails
3	8	0.08m	moderate	50-60%	18+	u	N/S	extended, supine	broken rib, fused toes	
3	10	0.05m	poor	5-10%	18+	u	-	-		
3	R2	-	moderate	75-80%	26-35	f	N/S	extended, prone		17 Fe coffin nails. c. 55 hobnails by left knee

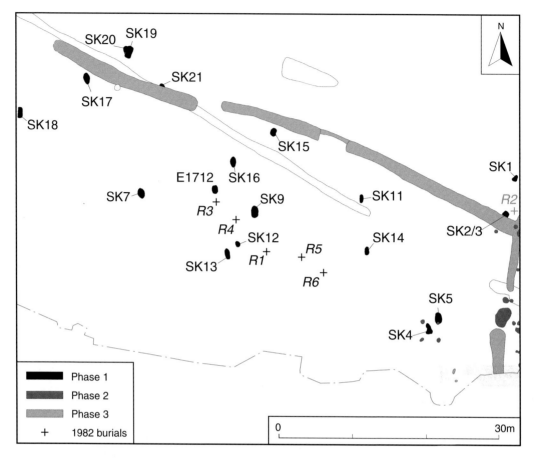

Fig. 4: Plan of cemetery showing Phase 1 inhumations (scale 1:500)

associated with these burials was a Middle/Late Iron Age finger ring lying in the space between the left humerus and ribs of SK9. It was not clear if the ring had been deliberately placed in this location during burial or whether it had originally been suspended around the neck on a cord and slipped into this position during post-burial settlement.

Phase 2

A series of stone-packed postholes and small pits was uncovered in the south-eastern corner of Area A, where modern truncation had been less severe; it is likely that similar features elsewhere have been destroyed. These pits and postholes were fairly irregular in plan and 0.1–0.3m deep, with the largest pit (289) being 2.7m across (Fig. 7). While eight of these features contained Middle Iron Age pottery, four yielded mid or later 1st-century AD material, suggesting some overlap between this phase and Phases 1 and 3. Some of the pits contained animal bones, charcoal and cess-like material suggestive of the disposal of domestic waste. Fragments of burnt daub exhibiting clear rod/wattle impressions were also recovered from some of these features; particularly pit 130 and postholes 126 and 132, suggesting that at least one structure stood in the vicinity. Also probably attributable

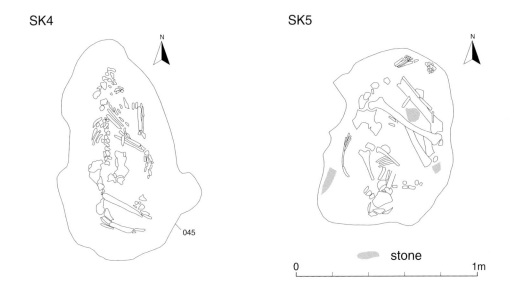

Fig. 5: Plan of SK4 and SK5 (scale 1:20)

Fig. 6: Intercutting crouched inhumations SK19 and SK20, looking west (scale 30cm)

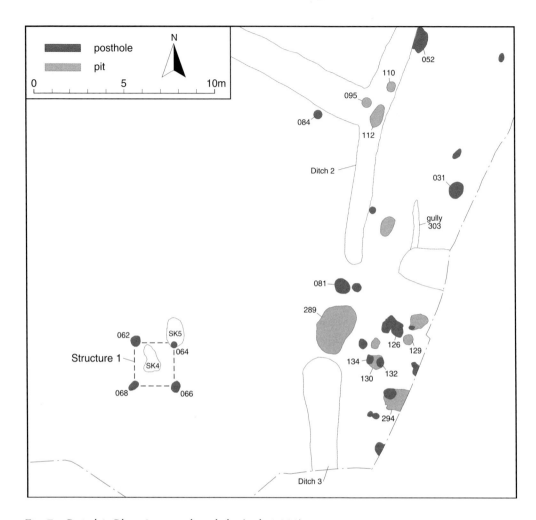

Fig. 7: Period 1, Phase 2 pits and postholes (scale 1:200)

to this phase of activity is a 2.5m-length of highly truncated gully (303) that was cut by features attributable to later phases.

The majority of these pits and postholes were located to the east of Enclosure 1 and Ditches 2 and 3 (see Phase 3, below) and did not represent any clear structures. However, four postholes (062, 064, 066 and 068) situated approximately 7m west of Ditch 3 formed a distinct structure measuring approximately 3m square (Structure 1; Fig 7). The postholes were between 0.35m and 0.65m in diameter and 0.2m to 0.35m deep. Each contained a single silty clay fill and the remnants of post-packing stones. Although posthole 064 cut Phase 1 inhumation SK5, Structure 1 appears to be centred on Phase 1 inhumation SK4. This may indicate that the feature was a superstructure of some form, constructed to 'mark' the inhumation. Alternatively the location of the feature over the inhumation may have occurred entirely by chance, with the structure being related to the pits and postholes to the east of Ditch 3.

Phase 3

Enclosure 1 was rectilinear in shape, *c.* 70m long by 40m wide, with its long axis orientated north-west/south-east (Fig. 3). It was defined by a series of ditches (Ditches 1, 4, 5 and 6), Ditch 1 being up to 2m wide and over 1m deep, although it became considerably narrower and shallower as it approached the southern corner of the enclosure. The ditch was of irregular profile, a consequence of having been dug through the limestone bedrock. In two locations on the south-eastern and south-western sides of the enclosure evidence for the recutting of Ditch 1 was found, which did not relate to any of the later modifications discussed below. In the main, however, the ditch appeared to have been dug as a single episode. It is probable that the fragments of bedrock dug from the ditch were used to construct a bank immediately inside the ditch, and this is supported by the composition of the ditch fills. Ditch 1 typically contained three fills (Figs 8a and 8b), with primary silt 227 accumulating whilst the ditch was open. Secondary fill 226, which was very stony, appears to be the result of deliberate backfilling with bank material. Tertiary fill 218 probably resulted from further silting of the remaining hollow during later activity at the site (see Period 2, below).

Ditches 5 and 6 continued the alignment of Ditch 1 to complete the boundary of Enclosure 1 on its south-western side. These ditches were on average 1.5m wide and up to 0.7m deep with a fairly irregular profile and up to three stony infills. Once again it is likely that the material excavated from these ditches was in a bank that was subsequently slighted into the ditches. Two breaks between the ditches, each 3m to 4m wide, served as entranceways into the enclosure. Shallow Ditch 4, no more than 0.4m deep, bridged the gap between Ditches 1 and 5 and served as a drainage gully or culvert across the entranceway. Ditches 1 and 6 cut across burials SK2/3 and SK21, indicating that Enclosure 1 was later than these burials, and unlikely to be contemporary with any of the inhumations, which occur both inside and outside of the enclosure. Additionally, SK1 and SK19/20 were in locations which would have been occupied by the internal bank, further indicating that the enclosure was built without reference to the earlier burials. On face value Enclosure 1 is unusual, as it does not contain any internal features. However, this can probably be attributed to the especially high degree of modern truncation present in this area of the site, and it is likely that such features did once exist.

Two further ditches (Ditches 2 and 3) ran southwards from the southern corner of Enclosure 1 (Figs 3 and 7). They may have defined an annexe or close attached to the enclosure, the 5m-wide gap between the ditches serving as an entrance. The ditches were *c.* 1.5m wide and up to 0.6m deep and each contained a single stony silt fill yielding pottery of similar date to that retrieved from the backfills of the Enclosure 1 ditches. With the exceptions of posthole 084, Structure 1 and four features cut by Ditch 1 (pits 110 and 112 and possible postholes 052 and 095), the postholes and pits ascribed to Phase 2 lay to the east of Ditches 2 and 3 and Enclosure 1. As four of these features contained mid or later 1st-century AD pottery it is likely that they overlap Phases 2 and 3. It is therefore possible that the ditches formed a western boundary to the activity reflected by the postholes and pits, perhaps representing the formalisation of the landscape after an initial period of open occupation. However, it is possible that further postholes and pits once extant to the west of the ditches have been removed by later truncation; it is significant that the ground level dropped from approximately 39.8m AOD in the region of pit 289 to 37.9m AOD by Phase 1 inhumation SK18.

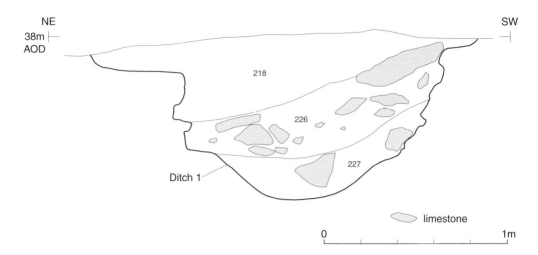

Fig. 8a: Ditch 1 (north), section (scale 1:20)

Fig. 8b: Ditch 1 (north), section, looking north-west (scales 1m)

The dating evidence for Period 1, by E.R. McSloy

Viewed overall, the Period 1 pottery represents a relatively homogeneous assemblage, largely comprising calcite-tempered wares typical of the Late Iron Age and 1st century AD in this region. Small quantities of material from certain pits and postholes appear to be representative of slightly earlier (Middle Iron Age) activity. Mid or later 1st-century AD (probably pre-Flavian) dating is suggested by the wheel-thrown, 'Belgic' style vessels in calcitic and grogged fabrics which occur in Ditches 2–6 and in pit 112. Romanised oxidised and reduced wares also occur in forms suggestive of similar dating.

Phase 1 burials

The crouched arrangement of these burials is a feature of prehistoric inhumations over a lengthy period. Middle Iron Age or earlier dating for at least one grave (SK5) is suggested by its being cut by posthole 062 of Structure 1, the fill (061) of which yielded a small quantity of Middle Iron Age pottery. Scraps of pottery in calcareous and sandy fabrics were recovered from grave fills of SK5 and SK16. One sherd from deposit 209, the fill of SK16, preserved a burnt food residue from which a radiocarbon determination was obtained (Wk-18620: 2722 +/- 32 BP) which calibrates at 95% confidence to 930–800 cal. BC (see *the radiocarbon dates*, below). This suggests a Late Bronze Age date. Later dating is suggested by the one grave good from the cemetery, the finger ring associated with SK9, the best parallels for which date from the Middle or Later Iron Age. Considering that the dated residue was recovered from a thumbnail-sized scrap of prehistoric pottery, it is most likely that this sherd is a residual Late Bronze Age artefact incidentally introduced into the grave fill, and so the Mid to Late Iron Age date for the burials suggested by the finger ring is to be preferred.

Phase 2

Several features, including the fills of postholes 031, 081, 132, 134, and 062 (part of Structure 1), and pits 129, 130 and 294, produced small but compositionally distinct groups attributable to the Middle Iron Age. Coarse shelly, limestone-tempered or sandy fabrics dominate, with fewer calcitic fabrics compared to later groups described below. Forms consist of barrel-shaped jars with simple or squared rims, which find parallels in Middle Iron Age groups in the region and beyond. Posthole 84 and pits 95, 112 and 289 produced generally consistent material, with calcite-tempered fabrics prominent and including wheel-thrown vessel forms (Fig. 13.9 and 13.14) firmly suggestive of mid or later 1st-century AD dating.

Phase 3

Pottery from ditches forming Enclosure 1 amounted to 313 sherds or approximately 86% of the Period 1 assemblage. Most pottery derived from upper fills with only 20 sherds recovered from lower or primary deposits. The basal fills of Ditch 1 (049 and 089) contained bead-rimmed jars in calcitic fabrics and a grog-tempered sherd probably indicating a date not before the middle of the 1st century AD.

Handmade vessels in calcite-tempered wares dominate the remainder of the assemblage, with bead-rim jars most characteristic (Table 3). A date between the Late Iron Age, perhaps the 1st century BC, extending to the Early Roman period (1st century AD) is applicable for this material on the basis of excavated parallels across the west of Britain and south Wales. A date towards the later part of this range, *c.* AD 50–80, is indicated by a small number of wheel-thrown forms in calcitic, grog-tempered and 'Romanised' oxidised or reduced sandy fabrics. Forms include 'Belgic'-style necked jars and bowls (Fig. 13.13) and a butt-beaker copy (Fig. 13.12). Savernake ware, the only material of non-local origin present, is dateable from the mid 1st to earlier 2nd century AD. An abraded sherd of greyware from lower fill (049) of Ditch 1 and a sherd of central Gaulish samian from its secondary infill (183) can be regarded as intrusions.

Period 2: Roman (2nd to early 3rd century AD) (Fig. 9)

Phase 4

The ditches of Enclosure 1 were at least partially backfilled with redeposited bank material in the 1st century AD. The resulting hollow gradually silted up during the following century with several sherds of late 2nd to early 3rd-century AD pottery recovered from the upper silts. Following the abandonment of Enclosure 1 and its possible annexe defined by Ditches 2 and 3, a new ditch (Ditch 7) was dug following the general alignment of the south-eastern side of Ditch 1. It is likely that the alignment of Ditch 7 was influenced by the denuded remains of the internal bank on the south-eastern side of Enclosure 1, and possibly a similar bank on the western side of Ditches 2 and 3. After running north-east for 32.5m, Ditch 7 turned to the south-east and ran out of the area of excavation. It was 1.6m wide and 0.25m deep with a single silty fill. Ditch 7 enclosed an area largely outside of the eastern limit of excavation, and no internal features that are securely contemporary with it were recorded, although posthole 337 lay adjacent to the ditch near the southern limit of excavation. As this posthole cut the final infill of Ditch 3 it may belong to the same phase of activity as Ditch 7. If this posthole is indeed associated with the ditch, then it has repercussions for the location of any internal bank.

An isolated pit (155) lay within the bounds of Enclosure 1. It was up to 1.8m wide, 0.46m deep, with a 'U'-shaped profile and contained two silty fills (153 and 154). Both fills yielded fragments of arm bones from a neonatal human skeleton. The sherds of pottery and flecks of charcoal also present suggest that this was a rubbish pit that had been used for the disposal of human remains rather than a specifically excavated grave. Irregular pits 364 and 366, 0.6–0.7m deep, lay near the northern limit of excavation and contained similar fills including quantities of pottery and animal bone indicative of rubbish disposal. Immediately to the west of these pits was a 10m-length of shallow gully (370).

Phase 5

Features assigned to this phase contained artefacts of similar date to those of Phase 4 and the two phases are likely to be broadly contemporary, despite Phase 5 features cutting some of those in Phase 4. In the north-western part of Area A, Ditches 8 and 9 and gully 350 formed two sides of a rectilinear enclosure (Enclosure 2). Ditch 8 was up to 0.9m wide and 0.5m deep and became increasingly truncated as it ran north-eastwards. It had a fairly flat base and contained a single clayey fill with frequent limestone inclusions. This stone may indicate that, as with Enclosure 1, spoil excavated from the ditch formed an internal bank which was later employed as backfill material. Gully 350, 0.3m wide, curved from the north-western terminus of Ditch 8 towards Ditch 9, forming the north-western corner of Enclosure 2. It is not clear if a 4m-wide gap between gully 350 and Ditch 9 was an entrance or merely the result of truncation. Ditch 9 was also highly truncated, surviving to a depth of only 0.08mm. It is possible that the north-west side of Enclosure 2 was defined by Ditch 14, 1.3m wide and 0.6m deep with a 'V'-shaped profile. Only a limited length of this ditch was examined due to truncation by Period 3 features. The alignment of Enclosure 2 mirrored that of Enclosure 1. Ditch 8 respected the north-western terminal of Ditch 1, serving to close off the apparently unmarked north-western side of Enclosure 1. This suggests that Enclosure 1 was still a visible landscape feature at this time.

As with Enclosure 1, internal features within Enclosure 2 were sparse, possibly due to truncation. Gully 13, up to 0.4m wide and 0.1m deep, contained a single silty deposit and

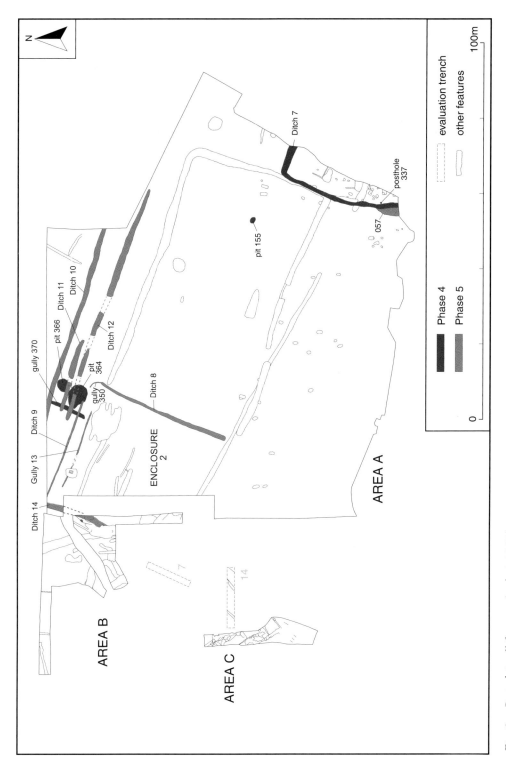

Fig. 9: Period 2, all features (scale 1:1000)

ran parallel with Ditch 9 for a distance of 22m (an ephemeral length of gully disturbed by a modern manhole probably belongs to the same feature and it is likely that it was originally continuous). Gully 13 might have channelled run-off from the rear of the conjectured internal bank of Enclosure 2, which therefore would have been up to 3m in width. To the north-east of Ditch 9 lay three parallel ditches (Ditches 10, 11 and 12) which shared the alignment of Enclosure 2. Again, modern truncation was extensive and these features survived to a maximum depth of only 0.2m. Their average width was 1.3m and all three ditches contained similar silty clay fills. Ditches 10 and 12 may have defined a trackway 4.4m wide, but the function of the intermediate Ditch 11 is unclear. Pre-truncation Ditch 11 might have been a replacement of the southern boundary of the trackway.

In the south-east corner of the site a 0.25m-thick silty spread (057) contained quantities of animal bone and pottery consistent with a date within Period 2. It overlay infilled Ditch 7 and presumably represents waste derived from nearby occupation.

The dating evidence for Period 2, by E.R. McSloy

Phases 4 and 5

Much of the pottery from these features occurs in small groups with few specific date markers. These are mainly provided by sherds of Central Gaulish samian and in some instances by Dorset Black-Burnished ware (hereafter BB1), mostly jar or bowl forms typical of the period c. AD 120/40–220/40. Attribution to this period is in some instances largely on stratigraphic grounds and/or the absence of specifically earlier or later types. Pit 364 produced the largest and best-dated pottery group from Period 2 (101 sherds). The assemblage was dominated by greywares but also included two sherds of Central Gaulish samian including a Drag. 27 cup dateable to c. AD 130–60. Corresponding dating is likely for a BB1 flat-rimmed dish with lattice decoration (as Gillam 1976 type 57). The greywares are heavily influenced by BB1 styles current in the 2nd and early 3rd centuries AD and include everted-rim jars and a bead-rim dish.

A single coin and several items of metalwork correspond with the date-span of Period 2, but only one of these artefacts was stratified in a Period 2 context. This was a T-shaped brooch from fill 361 of Ditch 12, which dates to c. AD 70–150. A denarius of Hadrian and a trumpet-derivative brooch of 2nd-century AD date are residual finds within Period 3 contexts, and a hinged T-shaped brooch is unstratified.

Period 3: Late Roman (later 3rd to 4th centuries AD) (Figs 10 and 11)

Phase 6 (Fig. 10)

The denuded remnants of the bank and partially infilled ditches of Enclosure 1 evidently remained a visible feature in the landscape as two lengths of severely truncated ditch (Ditches 21 and 22) containing Late Roman pottery formed an internal division across the centre of Enclosure 1. Four graves containing extended inhumation burials orientated roughly north/south (R2, SK6, SK8 and the heavily truncated SK10) were dug to the south of Ditch 22. R2 was buried prone (face down), whilst the other burials were supine. Burial SK6 also included the incomplete remains of a neonatal infant, some animal teeth, and the presence of iron nails with this burial and R2 indicate that they were buried in wooden coffins. A group of about 55 iron hobnails associated with dark staining by

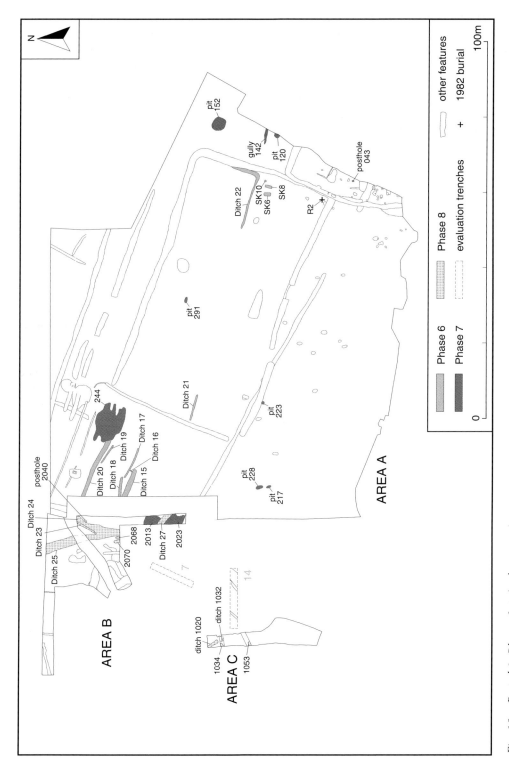

Fig. 10: Period 3, Phases 6–8 (scale 1:1000)

the left knee of R2 suggest that nailed footware had been placed in this position within the grave. Three pieces of limestone had been placed between the elbows and pelvis as though to keep the lower arms in position; other apparently placed stones lay below the left tibia, between the ankles and around the skull (Russell 1983, fig. 2). The small amount of pottery from the grave fills of SK6 and SK8 could only be broadly dated to the 2nd to 4th centuries AD, but these inhumations are typical of late Roman practice and are distinct from the Period 1 crouched burials.

Heavily truncated Ditches 15–20 were found in the north-western corner of Area A within the bounds of Enclosure 2. Parallel Ditches 15 and 20, 9.5m apart, shared the same alignment as Enclosure 2. The ditches were 1.2–1.4m wide with a single silty fill, and survived to a maximum depth of 0.25m. Between these ditches lay four very ephemeral features (Ditches 16–19), *c.* 0.4m wide and 0.1m deep. Ditches 15 and 20 might be the severely truncated boundaries of a trackway that replaced the Period 2 trackway, with the minor features representing wheel ruts. However Ditches 15 and 20 did not continue westwards into Area B, which, if not due to truncation, counters this interpretation. Another possibility is that Ditches 15 and 20 were drip gullies along the sides of a rectangular timber building, with the shallower features serving as beam slots (see *discussion*, below).

Phase 7 (Fig. 10)

Ditch 20 was partially overlain by a 0.1m-thick silty spread (244) containing abundant fragments of animal bone and pottery. Similar Late Roman deposits (2013 and 2023) were recorded in the southern part of Area B, and it is likely that they all represent spreads of domestic waste. An isolated pit (152) was examined in the north-east corner of Area A. It was 4m in diameter, and was excavated to a depth of 1.2m without the base being exposed. Its sequence of fills indicated that it had gradually silted up over an extended period of time before it was backfilled with stony material. The rubble was sealed by a layer of domestic waste (151) containing abundant animal bone and pottery. The pit may have been a watering hole that was employed for the disposal of rubbish once it fell out of use. Another pit (223) cut into the southern edge of Ditch 6. It was 0.8m in diameter, 0.2m deep, and its fill (222) included disarticulated fragments of human bone. The small size of the pit and the absence of domestic refuse differentiate it from Phase 4 pit 155, which also contained human remains. The human remains in this pit were perhaps disturbed from a Period 1 burial. Two further refuse pits (217 and 228) lay adjacent to each other towards the western limit of Area A. Other discrete features attributed to this phase in Area A but too insubstantial and truncated to be usefully characterised include pits 120 and 291, posthole 043, and gully 142.

Phase 8 (Fig. 10)

Activity in the later phases of Period 3 was mainly concentrated in Areas B and C, indicating a general shift of activity to the west of Enclosures 1 and 2. Area B contained a complex of ditches that, unlike those in Area A, did not generally follow the alignments of Enclosures 1 and 2. In the southern part of Area B, Phase 7 occupation deposits 2013 and 2023 were cut by 1.5m-wide Ditch 27 while a further three ditches (Ditches 23, 24 and 25) lay in the eastern half of the area. Each contained similar silty fills, had 'U'-shaped profiles, and presumably served to drain this wet part of the site. An undated posthole (2040) lay immediately to the east of Ditch 23, and the two may have been associated. Ditch 23 was

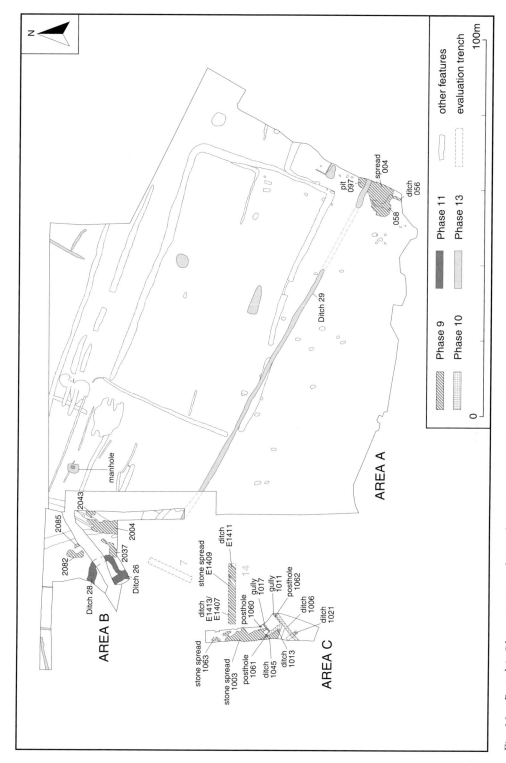

Fig. 11: Period 3, Phases 9–11, and Period 4: Phase 13 (scale 1:1000)

recut by Ditch 24, which also cut the western edge of posthole 2040. Ditch 25 was on a different alignment to Ditches 23 and 24 but the three ditches merged together as they headed south. It was not possible to determine their relationships due to the similarity of their fills. Two other short lengths of gully (2068 and 2070) were found in Area B but their function remains unclear.

Area C contained a number of clayey make-up layers (1010, 1031, 1048). These, in combination with the relatively high degree of modern disturbance present in the south and eastern parts of the excavation trench, served to obscure any earlier features. These deposits were not fully excavated but a series of sondages revealed that they sealed a number of shallow Later Roman ditches (1020, 1032, 1034) and a pit 1053.

Phase 9 (Fig. 11)
In the south-east corner of Area A the site a roughly 'L'-shaped feature (058) was cut into Period 2 occupation spread 057. Its plan and irregular profile indicate that this was not a foundation trench for a stone wall but rather a ditch which was deliberately backfilled with limestone fragments set in a clay matrix. A pit (097) lay 4.5m to the north-east of feature 058. The pit was cut by later features and extended beyond the limit of excavation but was 0.45m deep and in excess of 2.75m wide with a flattish base (Fig. 12). It was infilled with a similar stone deposit to ditch 058. These features were partially sealed by 0.2m-thick stony layer 004. Measuring up to 10m wide, this deposit was irregular in plan and consisted of limestone fragments set in a clay matrix. It is likely that the infilling of ditches 058 and 097 with stone and the deposition of this overlying layer happened as part of the same

Fig. 12: Period 3, Phase 9 pit 097, looking south (scale 1m)

episode, which coins and pottery from layer 004 suggest occurred *c.* AD 270–300. The rubble deposit also contained quantities of iron slag and numerous fragments of pennant roof tile fragments, which suggest that it was demolition rubble collected from a structure external to the excavation area. The edge of stone spread 004 was cut by (or possibly respected by) ditch 056, which ran southwards out of the excavation area.

Similar stony deposits were recorded in Areas B and C. The disused Phase 8 ditches in Area B were partially overlaid by a series of amorphous stone spreads (2004, 2037, 2043, 2082 and 2085). Spread 2004 sat on a 0.2m-thick clay silt bedding layer 2028. In Area C stone spread 1003 was exposed to a width of 4m; it had been truncated by later disturbance and it is likely that isolated patch 1063 formed part of the same feature. As with stone spread 004 in Area A, stone spread 1003 included quantities of iron slag. The stone spread lay on a series of make-up layers of redeposited natural, 0.2–0.5m thick, which sealed the Phase 8 features in this area. It is likely that this material was deposited in an attempt to raise the ground level to counter the high level of the water table in this part of the site. The limit of stone spread 1003 was defined on its south-east side by gully 1017, and on its south-western side by ditch 1045 which was difficult to discern in plan, becoming impossible to trace as it ran south-west into the more highly disturbed region of Area C. A section excavated across ditch 1045 revealed that it was the recut of an earlier ditch (1036). Gully 1017 was 0.5m wide and ditch 1045 was 2m wide; both contained silty clay fills. Although the stone spreads in Areas A, B and C appeared to have been deliberately levelled off to create surfaces they were very irregular in plan and did not define specific wall lines. It is possible that they acted as bases upon which timber-framed buildings were erected (see *discussion*, below). In this case ditches 1017 and 1045 might have provided drainage around two sides of a structure sat upon 1003. A similar sequence was recorded in evaluation trench 14, which lay immediately east of Area C (Fig. 11). Here, stony deposit E1409 (initially interpreted as a road surface in the evaluation) was flanked by ditches 1411 and 1413/1407. To the south of the stone spreads was drainage ditch 1021, near the south-western limit of Area C. It contained a series of three silty fills and was recut by Phase 10 ditch 1006.

Phase 10 (Fig. 11)

Gully 1017 in Area C was cut at its south-west end by ditch 1013 which replaced ditch 1045. Another gully 1011 was dug at right angles to 1017 and both it and ditch 1013 were filled with limestone fragments set in a clay matrix. Their function is unclear, but it is interesting to note that gully 1011 and ditch 1013 seem to define the south-east and south-west sides of the possible structure indicated by the Phase 11 postholes (below). Once again the Phase 10 features appear to be stone-filled ditches rather than foundation trenches, but their ephemeral and truncated nature and the absence of any basal silting means that it is difficult to be certain of their original form. Part of a similar stone-filled ditch (E705) containing 3rd to 4th-century AD pottery was recorded in evaluation Trench 7. Lying immediately to the south-east of gully 1011 was another drainage or boundary ditch (1006).

Phase 11 (Fig. 11)

Three stone-packed postholes (1060, 1061 and 1062) in Area C cut into the infills of ditches 1006 and 1013 and gully 1011. They may have been part of a timber structure of some description. Two stone-filled ditches lay in the south-west corner of Area B. Ditch 26 was 0.6m deep. It contained a 0.2m-thick basal silting sealed by a 0.3m-thick deposit of large limestone fragments set in silt that was in turn covered by a 0.25m-thick layer of fragmented limestone. The secondary fill of Ditch 26 contained the largest concentration of ironworking slag recovered from any one feature at the site. Immediately to the north-east of Ditch 26, Ditch 28 curved away in a rough 'U' shape. It contained a similar deposit of fragmented limestone deposit resting on 0.2m of primary silt. Although these two ditches joined together as they headed south, the relationship between them could not be established. It is clear that these features were not excavated as foundation trenches. The basal silts show that they remained open for a period after excavation, perhaps as drainage features, and were infilled with limestone once they had gone out of use. In this they are similar to the Phase 9 stone-filled features 058 and 097, indicating that this process was an ongoing one at the site. These ditches may have been backfilled as preparation for the construction of a foundation raft for a building, all trace of which has been destroyed.

Phase 12 (not illustrated)
The features in Areas B and C were covered by a thin (0.1m to 0.2m-thick) layer of reddish grey silty clay (2002, 2007, 1029 and 2003), the latter including a high frequency of ironworking slag. These deposits might represent a ground surface that formed after the cessation of occupation in these areas, or possibly the remains of levelled cob walls which sat upon the possible building rafts. Similar layers were recorded in evaluation trenches 7 (E706) and 14 (E1405).

The dating evidence for Period 3, by E.R. McSloy

Area A
A broad later Roman date can be ascribed for certain features in Area A mainly on the basis of pottery coarsewares. The fills of Phase 6 Ditches 15, 16, 17, 18, 19 and 20 and Phase 7 waterhole 152 produced small but consistent pottery groups. Pottery from these features typically comprised reduced wares, predominantly a mix of greywares (c. 60% by count) consistent with types produced at Congresbury, North Somerset, between the late 2nd and 4th centuries AD (Bennett 1985; Sabin 2000) and BB1 forms typical of the 3rd and 4th centuries AD. The small quantities of pottery recovered from the grave fills of burials SK6 and SK8 are only broadly dateable to the period between the 2nd and 4th centuries AD.

Nine of the eleven coins from the Phase 9 artefact-rich stone spread 004 are radiates of the period c. AD 260–95, including issues of AD 270–3. A worn denarius of Hadrian from this context is residual and a *Gloria Excercitus* issue is probably an intrusion. A further radiate of Gallienus (c. AD 260–8) was recovered from underlying rubble layer 114. Pottery from layer 004, which amounted to 174 sherds, included a substantial (residual) 1st-century AD component. The remainder, however, is consistent with the dating of c. AD 270–300 indicated by the coins. The bulk of this material consists of BB1 and local sandy reduced wares, including forms imitating BB1 types. BB1 forms comprise those typical of the 3rd century AD, in particular a substantially complete plain-rimmed dish with intersecting arc decoration (as Gillam 1976, nos 77–9), and those dating to after c. AD 240/50, which include conical flanged bowls and jars with obtuse-angled lattice decoration. Finewares include Central Gaulish samian including a rivet-repaired Drag. 33 cup, a single sherd of Central Gaulish black-slipped ware. Sherds of Oxfordshire red colour-coated ware (Young 1977, types C45 and C68) and New Forest type beakers were also present.

Areas B and C

A coin of AD 330–5 from Phase 8 Ditch 23 is the only identifiable and stratified coin from this part of the site. Additional typically 4th-century AD bronze issues were recovered from stone spread 1003 (Phase 9) and the fill of Ditch 1006 (Phase 10). An unstratified Theodosian issue from Area C is evidence for continuation of activity into the final decades of the Roman period. The Period 3 pottery from Areas B and C is generally of comparable character to that from Area A. Dating is again indicated primarily by coarseware forms in, or inspired by, BB1. Material of this type occurred in Ditches 26 and 27 and abundantly in spread 2023 and possible former ground surface 2007. Activity in this part of the site extended demonstrably later than that within Area A, continuing into the second half of the 4th century AD or beyond. Good evidence for this is present in the form of rosette-stamped or painted vessel forms in Oxfordshire red colour-coated ware (Young 1977, types C70 and C52), which occur in Phase 12 deposit 2002 and the fills of ditches 1045 (Phase 9) and Ditch 26 (Phase 11), and Late Roman shell-tempered ware from Phase 12 deposit 2007. The presence of the latter in the west of Britain is most often taken as evidence for dating after *c.* AD 360.

Period 4: post-medieval and modern (Fig. 11)

Phase 13

No features dating to between the Late Roman and post-medieval periods were identified. A long ditch (Ditch 29) crossing Area A and the southernmost tip of Area B contained a small amount of residual Roman pottery but corresponded with a field boundary first depicted on a map of 1831 accompanying an account of the boundaries of Westbury-upon-Trym in 1803 (Wilkins 1920).

THE RADIOCARBON DATES
by Sylvia Warman

Three samples of human bone from skeletons SK5, SK15 and SK19 were initially submitted for dating from the group of crouched burials. Unfortunately, once they had been prepared it was apparent that insufficient collagen was present to successfully date the material, and so they were abandoned. Alternative material for dating was selected in the form of a charcoal fragment from the grave fill of SK5 and a residue on a small potsherd found in the fill of the grave containing SK16.

The samples were processed during 2005 at the University of Waikato Radiocarbon Dating Laboratory, Hamilton New Zealand. For details of methods and equipment used see University of Waikato Radiocarbon Dating Laboratory (2006). The results are conventional radiocarbon ages (Stuiver and Polach 1977) and are given in Table 2. The unsuccessful samples are also listed. Simple calibrations of the results are given in Table 10. All have been calculated using the calibration curve of Stuiver *et al.* (1998) and the computer program OxCal 3.10 (Bronk Ramsey 2005). Date ranges cited in the text are those at 95% confidence level unless otherwise specified. Ranges are derived from the probability method (Stuiver and Reimer 1993).

The results of the radiocarbon dating programme are disappointing due to the lack of protein in the human bone samples. The charcoal from the grave of SK5 produced a modern date. The fact that so few fragments of charcoal were present in the grave fills and that they were all small in size suggests that a certain level of bioturbation/mixing had occurred, so that the material selected for dating was not contemporary with the feature from which it was recovered. The residue on the potsherd produced an unexpectedly early date, placing it in the Late Bronze Age. Usually dating of residues is a very reliable method, so the inference must be that the sherd of pottery (which was very small) was residual within the grave fill.

Table 2: Calibrated radiocarbon results

Laboratory No.	Type	Context no. (Skeleton/grave)	Material	Radiocarbon Age (BP)	Calibrated date range (at 2σ 95.4% confidence)
Wk-18238	radiometric	106 (SK5)	human femur	Failed	-
Wk-18239	radiometric	205 (SK15)	human tibia	Failed	-
Wk-18240	radiometric	236 (SK19)	human femur	Failed	-
Wk-18619	AMS	105 (Grave fill of SK5)	*Viburnum/cornus*	modern date returned (119.4 +/- 0.5 %M)	-
Wk-18620	AMS	209 (Grave fill of SK16)	Residue on potsherd	2722 +/- 32	930–800 cal. BC

THE HUMAN BONE
by Teresa Gilmore

Introduction

The remains of 21 inhumations were excavated. Arm fragments from a heavily truncated grave (E1712) were also found during the evaluation. Nine individuals (SK4–6, SK8, SK14, SK15–17 and SK19) were suitable for full detailed osteological analysis. The remaining twelve individuals were briefly assessed for age and sex. Descriptions of the palaeopathology have been restricted to those individuals who were analysed in more detail. Where possible, prevalence rates for the population have been noted. No detailed examination of the six burials recovered from the 1982 excavations was undertaken, but the age/sex data where recorded is included in Table 1 (p. 13) and in this report. A small amount of disarticulated bone was recovered from other features, including two neonate and several adult limb bones from two Roman pits.

Methodology

Sex was determined using morphological criteria and metric variation (Bass 1995; Brothwell 1981; Buikstra and Ubelaker 1994). The standard five-sex classification was used: male, ?male, unknown, ?female, female. No attempt was made to assign sex to juvenile individuals.

Juvenile age was determined using dental eruption (Van Beek 1983) and epiphyseal fusion (Schwartz 1995). Adult age was assigned by consideration of the skeletal parts present; dental attrition (Brothwell 1981), and auricular surface degeneration (Lovejoy *et al.* 1986). No pubic symphyses survive due to the high degree of fragmentation. The age categories that have been used are: neonate (around the time of birth); infant (following birth to one year); juvenile (1–12 years); adolescent (13–17 years); young adult (ya; 18–25 years); young middle adult (yma; 26–35 years); old middle adult (oma; 36–45 years); mature adult (ma; 46+ years); and adult (a; over the age of 18 but parts required for ageing not present). Pathology was determined by macroscopic inspection using criteria in Manchester and Roberts (1995) and Schwartz (1995). Non-metric variation was determined using criteria in Brothwell (1981). Only limited metric analysis was possible due to the fragmentary nature of the remains.

Preservation and completeness

A five-grade system was used to assess preservation: excellent, good, moderate, poor and very poor. Excellent preservation indicates little erosion or fragmentation to the bone surface and integral structure, with all features being easily determined. Very poor preservation indicates complete or practically complete erosion of the bone surface and severe fragmentation.

All skeletal remains present have been subjected to a degree of fragmentation. No long bones survive intact. The bone surface is in good condition, with little root etching and erosion. Fifteen individuals are moderately preserved, with large recognisable fragments, and the remaining seven individuals are poorly preserved (Table 1). Completeness is determined on a percentage basis depending on the amount of the skeleton present for analysis. The most complete skeletons are SK5 and SK15, with up to 90% present.

Age and sex

The skeletons comprise 1 unknown, 1 non-adult and 26 adults (Table 1). Thirteen of the individuals could not be aged beyond adult due to the high degree of fragmentation and incompleteness. The remaining fourteen individuals include one juvenile of 9–10 years, three young adults between 18 and 25 years, eight young middle aged adults between 26 and 35 years, and two old middle aged adults between 36 and 45 years. Two fragments of neonatal bone recovered from the grave fill of SK6 (a ?male) could have belonged to a neonate placed within the grave alongside the adult.

Sex determination was only undertaken on the adult individuals, of which 14 are sufficiently well preserved to allow a determination to be made. Eight are male (four males and four ?males) and six are female (three females and three ?females).

Stature and non-metric traits

No long bones survive intact within the assemblage and consequently very little can be said about the stature of the population. A few non-metric traits were observed which are recorded in the archive.

Degenerative joint disease

Spinal osteoarthritis is apparent in one individual, SK19. Two cervical articulation facets demonstrate severe porosity with holes greater than or equal to 2mm diameter and eburnation of the joint surface. There is slight osteophytic lipping along the inferior rims of the articulation facet. The right femoral head and acetabulum (hip joint) both demonstrate porosity and eburnation, with some cysts appearing on the femoral head. Unfortunately the joint survives only as fragments.

Trauma

Two individuals, SK6 and SK8, demonstrate possibly traumatic lesions. SK6 appears to have four fractured right rib midsections and SK8 has a fractured left rib midsection. The evidence suggests that although the rib fracture had taken place some time before death, at least one of the fractures had not reunited. Two toe phalanges (distal and mid) belonging to SK8 have fused together. The remaining three distal and two mid phalanges demonstrate extra bone growth on the plantar (underside). This extra bone growth could be a secondary result after a fracture. All the fractures appear to be well healed with no sign of infection.

The other traumatic injury is a probable trepanation in the forehead of SK17. However, due to the degree of fragmentation it is not possible to determine the method of trepanation, if indeed that is what it is.

Metabolic disease

Cribra orbitalia, the presence of a fine pitting of the orbital roof, is linked to childhood anaemia and tends to get remodelled as the individual ages into adulthood. This condition is apparent in one individual, SK17.

Infectious Disease

SK4 displays periostitis on the internal (visceral) surface on 44/93 rib midsection fragments.

The distal left femur displays periostitis on both the anterior and posterior surfaces. Lamellar bone (indicative of healing inflammation) is present towards the proximal edges of the lesion. The left tibia has been affected by periostitis, again on the distal third of the shaft, on the posterior surface. The tibia fragment appears to be flatter anteriorly-posteriorly and bowed medially. The leg infection is present around the joint, distal femur (knee) and distal tibia (ankle); this could be due to any type of non-specific or specific infection, but cannot be diagnosed because of the fragmentary nature of the skeleton. The rib infection was due to a lung infection, possibly tuberculosis or pneumonia.

Dental Pathology

The most commonly encountered form of pathology in this assemblage is dental, probably due to the poor preservation of the bones. Fourteen individuals have surviving dentitions, although commonly as loose teeth, and a total of 226 teeth were recovered. Calculus is present on 182 teeth; SK19 demonstrates the most severe case. A maxillary left third molar is present with significant concretions of calculus covering all sides, leaving the final 5mm of root clear. The occlusal surface has a covering of calculus leaving the molar cusps clear.

Dental caries are present in 13/226 (6%) of teeth, relating to SK6, SK8, SK16 and SK17. No dental abscesses are present. Antemortem tooth loss is only apparent in the mandible of one individual, SK19, with the loss of eight teeth. SK5 exhibits mild periodontal disease located around the left maxillary premolars and molars. Enamel hypoplasia is present on 64/226 (28%) of teeth from SK5, SK6, and SK14–17.

Discussion and Conclusions

The skeletons are all of adults with the exception of one unknown and one child aged 9–10 years (SK14). Where skeletons can be sexed, there is an even proportion of males and females. A wide range of pathology had been noted, including fractured ribs, spinal joint disease, cribra orbitalia and infectious disease. The high degree of fragmentation has made diagnosis of pathological conditions difficult and some conditions will have been missed due to the absence or fragmentation of the required bone parts.

The presence of dental enamel hypoplasia on the teeth of six individuals, including SK17, who also had cribra orbitalia, suggests periods of physical stress during childhood, such as malnutrition or disease. SK14, a child, is one of the individuals exhibiting these lines of hypoplasia on the teeth and it is possible that the condition that caused the lesions contributed to this child's death. Roberts and Cox (2003, 130) calculate that caries affected 19.1% of the Roman population of Britain. The Henbury population is consistent with this statistic, but the calculus rate is significantly higher than the average of 8.4% of individuals (Roberts and Cox, 2003, 131), with 81% of teeth affected. This could be due to the Henbury population not practising good dental hygiene.

Traumatic injuries were mainly present on the Period 3 burials, SK6 and SK8. One individual (SK4) had evidence for infectious disease, with periostitis affecting the ribs and the left leg.

Iron Age and Roman human remains are currently poorly studied in the Bristol region, so the Henbury population, which also displays a wide variety of pathology, is a significant addition to the palaeopathological record.

THE FINDS
by E.R. McSloy

The worked flint

Seventeen pieces of worked flint pieces were recovered. A full catalogue of this material is included in the archive. Six pieces are unstratified and the remainder is demonstrably residual, occurring in contexts attributable to all periods of the site's use. Little among this small group is readily dateable by form. Six blade-like removals, most of which are broken, are probably Mesolithic. A notched flake and two scrapers, one of crude discoidal 'button' type and a better-made and larger discoidal scraper, probably date to the Late Neolithic or Early Bronze Age. A similar date for the single retouched flake, eight flakes/ chips and three core fragment/shatter pieces is likely. Fully cortical flakes are absent and the debitage group most likely relates to tool manufacture or maintenance. The condition of the assemblage is poor and consistent with deposition long after manufacture. Raw material is largely of good quality, mostly grey-brown, flint. Small areas of cortex survive on five pieces and where present this is thick and/or unabraded, suggesting derivation outside of the region from a primary chalk or chalk soil source.

The Pottery

Full recording of pottery, including quantification by sherd count, minimum vessel and weight, was reserved for the Period 1 assemblage. The much larger Periods 2–3 assemblage was recorded in more rudimentary fashion, given the partial survival of features assigned to these periods and the consequent problems of interpretation. Quantification records and a summary report for this material are included in the archive.

The Period 1 assemblage amounts to 387 sherds (4.2kg), representing a minimum of 175 vessels. In addition, some 118 sherds belonging to fabric types characteristic of the Late Iron Age or Early Roman period were redeposited in later features. The condition of the pottery is good, with minimal loss of surfaces and calcareous inclusions preserved, and the average sherd weight is moderately high at 11g. With the exception of a small group exhibiting Middle Iron Age characteristics, Period 1 pottery dates to between the Late Iron Age and the Early Roman period, a span which can almost certainly be confined within the 1st century AD. By far the largest component comprises calcite-tempered 'native wares', of the type which are characteristic for the Bristol Channel-Severn estuary region (Allen 1998).

Assemblage composition: fabrics and forms
Fabrics: short descriptions

SHELL (SH)
SH1: Handmade. Common quantity of moderately sorted fossil shell (2–4mm). Irregular fracture with soapy surface feel. Buff or red-brown exterior surface and margin with grey interior and margin. *Quantity: count 60; min. vess. 20; weight 884g*
SH2: Handmade. Sparse quantity of well-sorted fine or medium fossil shell (0.5–1mm). Fine irregular fracture with soapy surface feel. Grey-brown throughout or with patchy red-brown exterior surface. *Quantity: count 10; min. vess. 10; weight 6g*

LIMESTONE (LI)
LI1: Handmade. Abundant, well-sorted rounded or sub-rounded oolitic limestone (most 0.5mm) with sparse

fossil shell inclusions 0.5–1mm. Fine irregular fracture with sandy surface feel. Grey brown throughout or with buff-coloured interior. *Quantity: count 4; min. vess. 4; weight 125g*

LI2: Handmade. Sparse, poorly sorted ?carbonifereous limestone inclusions (1–5mm). Fine irregular fracture with smooth surface feel. Brown exterior surface with dark grey core and interior. *Quantity: count 9; min. vess. 5; weight 65g*

CALCITIC (C)

C1: Handmade. Moderate to common angular calcite (0.5–1mm). Variable sub-angular limestone and other mineral/argillaceous inclusions. Fine irregular fracture, generally with smooth surface feel. Typically dark grey throughout or with red-brown internal surface and margin. *Quantity: count 215; min. vess. 107; weight 2187g*

C2: Wheelthrown, description otherwise as for C1. *Quantity: count 25; min. vess. 4; weight 172g*

IRON AGE SANDY (Q)

Q: Handmade. Common, well-sorted quartz (0.1–0.3mm). Dark grey throughout or with red-brown internal surface and margin. Finely irregular fracture, generally with sandy surface feel. *Quantity: count 12; min. vess. 6; weight 102g*

GROG (G)

G: Common dark grey sub-rounded grog (1–2mm). Dark grey throughout or with paler grey margins. Fine irregular fracture with soapy feel. *Quantity: count 37; min. vess. 10; weight 284g*

SAVERNAKE (SAV)

SAV GT: Fully described by Tomber and Dore (1998, 191). *Quantity: count 2; min. vess. 2; weight 213g*

ROMAN SANDY REDUCED (RS)

BS: Common, well-sorted fine/medium quartz (0.1–0.3mm). Dark grey surfaces and mid grey core. Sandy feel and fine fracture. *Quantity: count 1; min. vess. 1; weight 3g*

GW: Common, well-sorted fine/medium quartz (0.1–0.3mm). Grey surfaces with reddish margins and mid grey core. Sandy feel and fine fracture. *Quantity: count 1; min. vess. 1; weight 14g*

ROMAN OXIDISED (O)

OX: Rare, well-sorted fine/medium quartz (0.1–0.3mm). Pale orange throughout or with buff orange core. Smooth feel and fine fracture. *Quantity: count 8; min. vess. 4; weight 106g*

CENTRAL GAULISH SAMIAN (SAM)

LEZ SA: Fully described by Tomber and Dore (1998, 34). *Quantity: count 1; min. vess. 1; weight 4g*

Pottery from a group of features in the south-east corner of Area A amounting to 34 sherds (from 32 vessels: 280g), was distinct compositionally from the remainder of the assemblage (Table 3). Shelly, sandy and coarse limestone-tempered fabrics occur in this group, with calcitic fabrics considerably less well represented compared to later groups described below. The few identifiable forms in this group consist of ovoid/barrel-shaped jars with plain (Fig. 13.1) or squared (Fig. 13.2) rims, which can be compared to Middle Iron Age forms from nearby sites (ApSimon 1959, fig. 37, nos 33 and 36; Laidlaw 2002, fig. 10, no. 9) and the wider Cotswold-Severn region, including the Upper Thames Valley. The range of fabrics, with shelly and limestone-tempered types most abundant, compares to those identified among the large Middle/Late Iron Age assemblage from Hallen (ibid., 37) and a smaller, broadly contemporary group from Cribbs Causeway, Filton (Timby 1998). Represented fabrics appear to contrast with most likely earlier groups from Kings Weston Down and Blaise Castle (ApSimon 1959, 161).

The small size of this group makes refinement of its chronology problematical. Those aspects of fabric and form which compare to material from Hallen may support a date within the final two centuries BC which was considered most likely for that much larger assemblage (Laidlaw 2002).

Calcite-tempered fabrics are prominent in Period 1 feature groups, the bulk coming from

Table 3: Period 1 pottery fabrics as minimum vessel number (Min. Vess.) and weight (Wt) in grammes

	Phase 2: pits/postholes		Phase 3: Enclosure 1		other	
Fabric	Min. Vess.	Wt	Min. Vess.	Wt	Min. Vess.	Wt
SH1	12	127	7	734	1	23
SH2	6	36	4	27	-	-
L1	3	12	1	113	-	-
L2	2	17	2	45	-	-
C1	6	42	94	2116	8	32
C2	-	-	3	93	1	79
Q	3	46	3	56	-	-
G	-	-	10	284	-	-
SAV GT	-	-	2	213	-	-
BS	-	-	1	3	-	-
GW	-	-	1	14	-	-
OX	-	-	2	72	2	34
LEZ SA	-	-	1	4	-	-
Total	32	280	131	3774	12	168

the fills of Enclosure 1 (Table 3), and together making up 63% of the total (minimum vessel count). Calcite-tempered wares of this type are characteristic of the Middle and Late Iron Age/1st century AD in the region (Peacock 1969; Allen 1998). Forms represented here compare for the most part with those described by Allen from the Severn Estuary Levels (1984, fig 4). Most common are handmade globular or rounded jars with well-defined 'bead', short everted or triangular rims (Table 4), occurring in a variety of sizes (Fig. 13.2–7). The preponderance of bead-rim jars and of a small number of wheel-thrown vessels, including 'Belgic'-inspired necked bowls (Fig. 13.9), are suggestive of relatively late, probably mid/later 1st century AD dating for the group. Decoration of the kind seen with (a small minority of) calcite-tempered vessels elsewhere is not apparent in this assemblage, again perhaps a reflection of relatively late dating. Evidence for use with the calcite-tempered group is common in the form of sooting (six vessels) and internal carbonised residues (nine vessels), suggesting use for cooking. Such evidence was restricted to smaller-sized vessels (those with rim diameter within the range 140–180mm).

Shell-tempered pottery occurs throughout the Period 1 assemblage. A large, bead-rim jar in this fabric (Fig. 13.8), serves to demonstrate continued use of such fabrics in the latest Period 1 contexts. Grog-tempered 'Belgic'-type pottery makes up 5% of the Period 1 total (by minimum vessel count). Forms comprise necked bowls, including at least one vessel with prominent cordon at the base of its neck (Fig. 13.10). Comparable pottery occurs in probable earlier and middle 1st century AD contexts at Bagendon, Glos. (Clifford 1961) and at Cirencester in association with the Claudian/Neronian fort (Rigby 1982, 161–3). Similar material occurring in western Britain, for example in Worcestershire (Bryant and Evans 2004, 245–6) and South Wales (Manning 1993, 59) is usually considered to date to the period immediately following *c.* AD 43 and to be circulated by potters following in the path of the army at this time. A small quantity of Savernake ware, including a necked storage jar (Fig. 13.15), is the only certainly non-local ware stratified in Period 1.

Fully 'Romanised' fabrics are present in small quantities in Period 1, predominantly from

Table 4: Period 1 pottery forms by fabric group

Form	attribute	Fig. 13 nos.	Fabric group						
			SH	LI	C	Q	G	SAV	O
Butt-beaker	everted rim	12, 14	-	-	-	1	-	-	1
Jar: barrel-shaped	simple rim	1	-	1	-	-	-	-	-
	squared rim	2	1	-	1	1	-	-	-
Jar: neckless, rounded or angular body	bead rim	4-5	-	-	18	-	-	-	-
	short, everted rim	-	-	-	3	-	-	-	-
	short, upright rim	3	1	-	3	-	-	-	-
	triangular rim	-	-	-	1	-	-	-	-
Jar, large, rounded	bead rim	6-8	1	-	4	-	-	-	-
	out-curved rim	-	-	-	2	-	-	-	-
Jar, necked	-	-	-	-	-	-	-	-	1
	out-curved rim	-	-	-	-	-	-	-	1
Jar, necked, large	out-curved rim	15	-	-	-	-	-	1	-
Bowl, necked	out-curved rim	9, 10, 13	-	-	3	-	2	-	1
Bowl, cordoned	-	11	-	-	-	-	-	-	-
miscellaneous	Simple base	-	1	-	6	-	1	-	-
	Pushed-out base	-	-	-	1	-	-	-	-

Enclosure 1 (Table 3). Most abundant is oxidised fabric OX. The source of this material is unclear, however local origin seems likely on the basis of the common occurrence of similar types from Sea Mills (Bennett 1985; Timby 1987). Forms, which are in all instances indicative of Early Roman dating, include butt-beaker copies (Figs 13.12 and 13.14) and necked bowls (Fig. 13.13) with clear 'Belgic' affiliations. The vessel shown in Fig. 13.14 is a reasonably faithful copy of a Gallo-Belgic (Cam. 112) butt-beaker, and compares to a more complete vessel from Sea Mills (Bennett 1985, fig. 18, no. 20).

Discussion

The Period 1 assemblage represents a small but significant group, one of few well-stratified groups of this date and character from the Bristol region. Middle Iron Age dating is probable for a distinct group of calcareous or sandy types from a restricted number of contexts. The bulk of the remainder consists of handmade calcite-tempered wares, a tradition with its origins in the Middle/Late Iron Age and continuing in use into the Early Roman period. The main occurrence here of calcite-tempered pottery alongside relatively short-lived 'Belgic' type or Gallo-Belgic influenced vessel forms indicates that the bulk of this material dates to the immediately post-conquest period, probably *c*. AD 50–80.

With the exception of the small quantity of Savernake ware from East Wiltshire, the Period 1 pottery is probably all of fairly local origin. Calcite-bearing veins which might provide the source of the inclusions present in the calcite-tempered group occur in the Bristol-Mendips area. The results of petrographic studies undertaken on this class of pottery suggest that production was undertaken in a number of locations across the Bristol Channel-Severnside region (Allen 1998; Webster *et al*. forthcoming).

Aspects of the assemblage compare with broadly contemporary groups from a wide area. There is some overlap with the much larger but largely unstratified groups from Sea Mills. Dominance at Henbury of the utilitarian forms and a complete absence of contemporary continental finewares distinguish this assemblage from that of Sea Mills and probably demonstrate 'lower status' habitation.

Catalogue of illustrated sherds (Fig. 13)

1. Handmade barrel-shaped jar with plain rim, fabric L1. Fill of posthole 081, Period 1, Phase 2.
2. Handmade barrel-shaped jar with squared rim, fabric Q. Fill of posthole 132, Period 1, Phase 2.

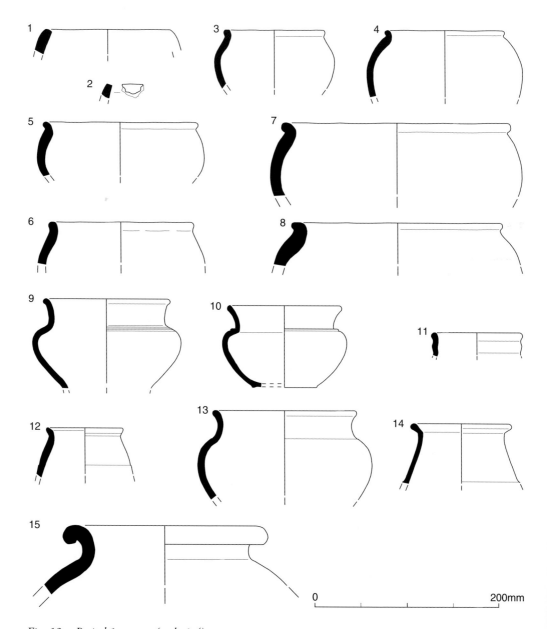

Fig. 13: Period 1 pottery (scale 1:4)

3. Handmade jar with angular profile and short, upright rim, fabric C1. Fill E605 of Ditch 1, Period 1, Phase 3.
4. Handmade jar, rounded/globular with bead rim, fabric C1. Fill E605 of Ditch 1, Period 1, Phase 3.
5. Handmade jar, rounded/globular with bead rim, fabric C1. Fill E605 of Ditch 1, Period 1, Phase 3.
6. Large handmade jar, rounded/globular with bead rim, fabric C1. Fill E605 of Ditch 1, Period 1, Phase 3.
7. Large handmade jar, rounded/globular with bead rim, fabric C1. Fill 091 of Ditch 1, Period 1, Phase 3.
8. Large handmade jar, rounded/globular with bead rim, fabric SH1. Fill E605 of Ditch 1, Period 1, Phase 3.
9. Wheel-thrown necked bowl with cordon, fabric C2. Fill of pit 095, Period 1, Phase 2.
10. Wheel-thrown necked bowl with cordon, fabric G. Fill E1709 of Ditch 5, Period 1, Phase.
11. Wheel-thrown cordoned/corrugated type vessel, ?bowl, fabric G. Fill E605 of Ditch 1, Period 1, Phase 3.
12. Wheel-thrown butt-beaker copy, fabric Q. Fill 098 of Ditch 4, Period 1, Phase 3.
13. Wheel-thrown necked bowl, fabric OX. Fill 070 of Ditch 3, Period 1, Phase 3.
14. Wheel-thrown butt-beaker copy, fabric OX with reddish orange colour wash. Fill 111 of pit 112. Period 1, Phase 2.
15. Large ?wheel-thrown necked jar, fabric SAV GT. Fill E610 of Ditch 2, Period 1, Phase 3.

The Roman coins

Eighteen coins were recovered (Table 5). The condition of all coins was poor, with the result that only one is fully identifiable.

Table 5: Coin catalogue (all Period 3)

Phase	Context	Denom.	Description	Date
7	pit 120 (fill 119)	AE3	urbs Roma. Wolf and twins. Mint illegible	AD 330–335
7	pit 120 (fill 119)	AE4	Illegible	C4
8	Ditch 23 (fill 2006)	AE3	Constantinopolis. Victory on prow with sceptre and shield. Mint illegible	AD 330–335
9	spread 004	Denarius	Hadrian. salus aug. RIC 46.	AD 117–38
9	spread 004	radiate	Victorinus. Pax standing l. with branch and transverse sceptre	AD 268–70
9	spread 004	radiate	Tetricus I. Spes holding up hem of dress. Holding flower and walking	AD 270–73
9	spread 004	radiate	Tetricus I. Reverse indistinct ?Fides	AD 270–73
9	spread 004	Barb. radiate	As Tetricus I? From Pax	AD 270–90
9	spread 004	?radiate	Illegible	AD 260–95
9	spread 004	Barb. radiate	As Tetricus I? From Pax	AD 260–95
9	spread 004	radiate	Illegible	AD 260–95
9	spread 004	?radiate	Illegible	AD 260–95
9	spread 004	AE3	Illegible	C4
9	spread 004	AE3	House of Constantine (obv. leg. uncert.). Gloria Exercitus (1 std). Lyon	AD 335–7
9	spread 114	Barb. radiate	Gallienus. From panther standing left	AD 260–68
9	spread 1003	AE4	Illegible	C4
10	ditch 1006 (fill 1007)	AE3	Illegible	C4
-	unstrat.	AE3	House of Theodosius. Victoria AUGGG Mint illegible	AD 388–402

The metalwork and worked bone

Ten items of copper alloy, 96 of iron (of which 81 are nails), one of lead and three of worked bone were recovered. Metal objects other than nails were examined in the conservation laboratory by x-radiography and their condition assessed. Iron items are extensively corroded, some are fragmented, and most have soil adhering. With the exception of less substantial items (the Aucissa-type brooch and tweezers), copper-alloy items have suffered minimal corrosion. Full details of these artefacts are contained in the archive. Selected artefacts of intrinsic interest are listed here.

Finger rings with overlapping terminals have been found in Middle to Late Iron Age contexts at Glastonbury (Bulleid and Gray 1917, pl. XLI), and Cadbury Castle in Somerset (Foster 2000, fig. 98). Exact parallels with one terminal featuring inscribed decoration are not forthcoming. The discontinuation of decoration at the ring's inner face supports the current functional interpretation, suggesting this was intended to be seen when worn. The finger ring accompanying SK9 (Fig. 14) was not worn at the finger, its position indicating it was placed at the chest region or worn as an amulet. A similar arrangement was noted on a considerably smaller form from Yorkshire (Stead 1991).

There are two brooches (not illustrated) of similar hinged T-shaped form, with enamelled and moulded lobate decoration to the bow. While they differ in detail, good parallels are known for each, for example nos. 12–15 and 19/21 among the large group of brooches from Nor'Nour, Isles of Scilly (Hull 1968, 31–3). The overall distribution of such brooches, which probably date to the latter part of the 1st or first half of the 2nd century AD, indicates south-western/south-central British manufacture (ibid., 34; Butcher 2001, 52).

Iron nails are listed in the archive. A group of 16 nails from the fill of SK6 are from a wooden coffin. Where complete, all nails conform to the common Roman Manning (1985, 134) 1B type, characterised by shaft 30–60mm long and plain flattened head. The iron knife fragments probably belong to Manning's (1985, 114) type 11(b), a form of knife common throughout the Roman period.

Catalogue of illustrated artefacts (Fig. 14)

Copper-alloy finger ring from round-sectioned rod. Oval in form with slightly overlapping terminals. One terminal is slightly expanded and decorated with ?three inscribed lines (to outermost areas only). Length 30.3mm; width 26.6mm. Rod diam. 3.4mm, expanding to 4.2mm at decorated terminal. Fill of grave 176 (SK9), Period 1.

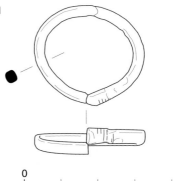

Fig. 14: *Period 1 copper-alloy finger ring, accompanying SK9 (scale 1:1)*

0   50mm

Non-illustrated artefacts

Copper-alloy Aucissa-type brooch. Extremely poor condition with very little of original surface surviving. Pin, catchplate, foot knob and much of hinge are missing. Bow is highly arched. Head, which is probably uninscribed, has at least two transverse mouldings. Dateable to mid 1st century AD. Length 43mm; width 17.4mm. Layer 244, Period 3.

Copper-alloy 'fly-shaped' trumpet brooch variant. Complete, except for the pin and a portion of the spring. The bow is flat, formed from expanding 'insect wings'. The upper portion has three channels for enamel, which only survives in the outermost where it is blue-green. There is an unpierced lug at the head and moulded 'tongued-form' foot-knob with collar above. Length 35.6mm; width 17.4mm. This item dates to the 2nd century AD but is residual within a 4th-century AD context. Brooches of this form are widely known, their distribution suggestive of no one area of manufacture or usage. From Ditch 26, Period 3.

Copper-alloy (with iron axis bar) T-shaped brooch. The upper part of the bow is distorted and the pin and a portion of the headloop are missing. An axis bar passes through tubular crossbar. The upper part of the bow, with two rectangular panels for yellowish enamel, is now mostly missing. The moulded decoration at the junction of the bow and foot consists of four lobes, the upper pair slanting with central groove, and joined to lower pair by a double groove. Small toe-knob with complex moulding. Length 62mm; width 28mm. Layer 361, Period 2.

Copper-alloy T-shaped brooch. Broken at a point below the junction of the bow and foot. A small portion of the is pin also missing. D-shaped, unperforated head-tab. The upper part of the bow, with two rectangular panels for greenish enamel, is now mostly missing. Moulded lobate decoration below enamel. Surviving length 25mm; width 18mm. Unstratified.

Two distorted portions of a copper-alloy cable bracelet from two strands of wire. Length (longest portion) 44mm; wire gauge 1.6mm. Published stratified examples invariably date to the Late Roman period, after *c.* AD 250 (Hooley 2001, 84). Area C, subsoil layer 1002.

A single arm from a pair of copper-alloy tweezers. From a narrow strip, tapering slightly towards the spring. Simple double incised line decoration, expanding from centreline at spring end. Surviving length 59mm; width at tip 5.5mm; width at break 3.7mm. A common Roman type. Similar simple decoration is known on examples of varying date (Hooley 2001, 109). Layer 004, Period 3.

Iron socketed tripod-form candlestick with expanding cup-like socket and bar-like S-shaped legs with short flattened feet (of which only one survives). The legs have been forged to form a bar-like stem. Length 136mm. Thickness at leg 7.2mm; at stem 8.4mm. Parallels for this item include examples from Portchester, Hampshire (Cunliffe 1975, 247, fig. 131, 249–50), and Nettleton (Wedlake 1982, fig. 96, no. 9) and Wanborough in Wiltshire (Isaac 2001, fig. 54, no. 218). Later Roman dating is indicated in all instances. Layer 004, Period 3.

Fragment of a round-sectioned shaft from an iron stylus, with small, chisel-like eraser. Surviving length 56mm, Diam. 55mm; shaft diam. 4.6mm; width of eraser 6mm. Manning's (1985, 85–7) type 1 or 2. Pit 366, Period 2.

Iron knife fragment. The tip and a portion of the tang are missing. Straight back with tang continuing line. Edge is convex rising towards tip. Surviving length 79mm; width 34mm. Ditch 1006, Period 3.

Iron with copper-alloy pommel cap. Knife fragments. Most of the blade is missing. Straight back with tang continuing line. A small area of convex edge survives. Oval pommel cap, cut from copper-alloy sheet. Surviving length 82mm; width 36mm. Ditch 26, Period 3.

Bone hairpin, Crummy type 2 dateable to *c.* AD 50–200/250 (Crummy 1979, 160–1). Point missing. It has a crudely worked conical head with single groove below. Highly polished. Surviving length 57.5mm; diam. 4mm, tapering to 3.2mm at break. Unstratified.

Lathe-made bone plano-convex spindlewhorl. Diam. 32mm; height 12mm; central perforation diam. 8mm; weight 10g. A relatively commonly encountered form, lathe-turned and probably adapted from the femoral head of a horse or cow. It compares to others of Roman date noted by MacGregor (1985, 187). Pit 152, Period 3.

Bone ?mount. Slightly curving and probably from the cortex of a large, (cattle-sized) longbone. 'Tongue-shaped' in plan with 'scalloped' upper edge. This is reduced on inner and outer faces. Running parallel with the upper edge is a row of four perforations. Single perforation centrally, close to rounded lower edge. Diam. 33mm; width at top edge 24mm; thickness 2.8mm. The function of this object is uncertain. Its tongue-shaped form and row of perforations to its upper (scalloped) edge is reminiscent of some Post-Roman strap ends (MacGregor 1985, fig. 60). The wear apparent to these perforations might be consistent with this interpretation and attachment with thread or similar material. Against this, the single perforation close to the rounded lower edge is not a functional feature of strap ends. Use as some form of decorative mount would appear to be most likely. Late Roman dating is suggested by associated pottery and coins. Layer 1003, Period 3.

The worked stone and building stone, by Fiona Roe

In addition to the fragment of rotary quern and spindlewhorl, some 40 fragments from roofing tiles were recovered, all of Pennant sandstone from the Upper Coal Measures which is readily available in the eastern part of Bristol. Pennant sandstone was widely used as a Roman roofing material on sites near the outcrops, as at Marshfield, South Gloucestershire (Barford 1985) and Shepton Mallet, Somerset (Leach with Evans 2001, 224).

Non-illustrated stone

Part of the upper stone from a Brandon Hill Grit rotary quern, well made, pecked to shape around the rim and on its upper surface. There is an indentation around the rim on the upper surface, and a slot for a handle. The grinding surface was pecked and then worn. Diam *c.* 360mm, thickness at rim *c.* 80mm. Brandon Hill Grit is a Carboniferous sandstone available in central Bristol. The only other example of a quern made from this material known to the author is from the Roman farmstead at Filwood Park, Bristol (Williams 1983, fig. 7, 4). Pit E703, unphased.

Disc-form lias spindlewhorl. Diam. 30mm; height 13.5mm; central perforation diam. 8mm; weight 18g. Pit 152, Period 3.

Fired clay and ceramic building material, by Sam Inder

Seventy fragments of fired or burnt clay weighing a total of 1042g were retrieved. The majority derived from Period 1 (44% by weight) and Period 3 (46%). Most of this consisted of small amorphous fragments or exhibited a single smoothed face. Fragments of burnt structural daub with clear rod/wattle impressions were most abundant in Period 1 contexts, with 413g recovered from the Period 1 (Phase 2) pit/posthole fills located in the south-west corner of Area A, particularly the fills of pit 130 and postholes 126 and 132.

Six fragments (95g) of ceramic building material were recovered from Period 2, 3 and later deposits. This material appears to be Roman, although its fragmentary and generally abraded condition prohibits full identification.

Metallurgical residues, by Sam Inder

Ironworking slag amounting to a total weight of 2069g was recovered from 20 contexts. All material consists of a moderately dense and blocky ironworking slag, with the bulk comprising relatively small fragments. None of the slag is identifiable to a specific process, with material of similar appearance produced by smithing and smelting. Approximately 60% of this material was either residual in post-medieval contexts or unstratified. Of the remainder only 78g was associated with Period 1 and 2 features, and the rest was from Period 3 features, specifically stone spreads 004 and 1003 in Areas A and C, and the infill of Ditch 26 and layer 2003 in Area B.

THE ENVIRONMENTAL EVIDENCE

Animal Bone, by Sylvia Warman

Animal bone from all periods was assessed (CA 2005) and it was recommended that the Period 1 material that was identifiable to species should be fully identified and published, while that collected from Periods 2 and 3 should be summarised. Details of each identified specimen are recorded on an Access database, available in the site archive, which contains full details of the methods used. In Table 6 two Minimum Number of Individuals (MNI) values are given. MNI added is the total if the separate feature totals are added together. MNI whole is for the entire Period, assuming individual animals could be incorporated into all types of feature. The latter values are therefore lower than the former. The MNI for each species is calculated in Table 7.

Table 6: Period 1 animal bone: count and weight by species

Species	No. bones	No. fragments	Weight (g)	MNI added	MNI whole
Cattle	36	44	1881	9	7
Dog	2	2	9	2	1
Horse	4	4	265	3	2
Sheep	11	11	208	3	2
Sheep/goat	27	45	249.5	8	5
Pig	9	10	133	2	2
Frog	1	1	0.25	1	1
Totals	*90*	*117*	*2745.75*	*28*	*20*

Period 1 results

The range of species present was small (see Tables 6–9), all domestic mammals apart from the frog limb found in a sample from Ditch 1. Cattle and sheep/goat make up the bulk of the identified material; sheep and pig are the next most numerous species, with horse and dog represented by just a few specimens in each case. The only species with clear evidence of both males and females was pig where canine teeth were identified (Schmid 1972).

Modification

A total of 21 specimens showed signs of butchery, mostly long bone shafts that had been chopped through. Almost half of the Period 1 specimens show the early stages of weathering but few show more advanced damage. Eight bones have been gnawed; seven by dogs. One, a horse cannon bone from Ditch 4, appears to have been gnawed by sheep (Brothwell 1976) and is identical to one viewed in the reference collection at the Institute of Archaeology, London. Three bones were burnt; all were black or grey black in colour indicating temperatures of 600–700° Celsius (Lyman 1994, 386).

Ageing

Due to too few multiples of the same element from each species (Table 8) it was not feasible to carry out ageing estimates based on long bone fusion. However a very young sheep/goat specimen from Ditch 4 appears to be a neonatal lamb (or kid). Reference to Prummel (1987) suggests an age of around 142 days gestation, very close to the usual time of birth.

Sheep/goat mandibles were relatively numerous so Mandible Wear Stage calculations following Grant (1975; 1982) were attempted. Most were identified as sheep/goat but one

Table 7: Period 1 animal bone: species totals by feature type

Feature type/species	No. bones	No. fragments	Weight (g)	MNI
Ditches and gullies				
Cattle	29	35	1378	5
Dog	1	1	6	1
Horse	3	3	241	2
Frog	1	1	0.25	1
Sheep	10	10	191	2
Sheep/Goat	23	40	239.5	7
Pig	9	10	133	2
Pits and postholes				
Cattle	4	4	218	1
Horse	1	1	24	1
Sheep	1	1	17	1
Sheep/goat	4	5	10	1
Layers				
Cattle	3	4	258	2
Graves				
Cattle	1	1	27	1
Dog	1	1	3	1
Totals	**90**	**117**	**2745.75**	**28**

individual had a lower fourth deciduous premolar (dp_4) which was clearly *Ovis* rather than *Capra* (following Payne 1985). The following Mandible Wear Stages were calculated from seven specimens: 8, 12, 23, 28, 28, 37, 42. This indicates that a range of ages is present, with a greater number of older individuals. With such a small sample it is not possible to comment further on the husbandry regime.

Summary of the results from Periods 2 and 3
This material was scanned and recorded during the assessment. A summary is provided in Table 9. Cattle are numerous throughout as are ovicaprids. Pig is present in smaller numbers with horse and dog represented by a handful of specimens. The material from Periods 2 and 3 is similar to that found at Sea Mills (Levitan 1985), not least the very small proportion that is fully identifiable (only 409 bones out of a total of 2327). The value of *c.* 18% can be compared to 24% of examples identifiable at Sea Mills.

Discussion of the Period 1 assemblage
The animal bone from Period 1 comprises a small number of mostly domestic species with a noticeable reliance on cattle and ovicaprids (sheep/goat). Pig, although present, is not numerous, and the feet and head elements may be the result of primary butchery rather than domestic waste. The only meat-bearing bone found was a single tibia. Dog and horse are present but only as a handful of bones, which probably represent a single dog and two horses. The finding of a horse cannon bone gnawed by sheep is interesting as this behaviour usually only occurs in individuals suffering dietary stress (Brothwell 1976) and may indicate some failures in the animal husbandry regime. Similarly the very young foetal/new born lamb or kid from Ditch 4 could be viewed as further evidence of poor livestock management, although a proportion of lambs will die however good their environment is. The sheep and sheep/goat

Table 8: Period 1 animal bone: by species and element

Species/element	Cattle	Sheep	Sheep/Goat	Pig	Horse	Dog	Frog
horncore	2	2	-	-	-	-	-
Skull	5	2	1	-	-	-	-
Maxilla	1	-	1	-	-	2	-
Upper teeth	3	-	1	1	1	-	-
Mandible	5	1	7	3	-	-	-
Lower teeth	-	-	5	3	1	-	-
Atlas	-	-	1	-	-	-	-
Humerus	1	1	1	-	-	-	-
Radius	3	2	1	-	1	-	1
Ulna	1	-	-	-	-	-	-
Metacarpal	5	-	1	-	1	-	-
Innominate	-	-	1	-	-	-	-
Femur	1	1	-	-	-	-	-
Patella	-	-	1	-	-	-	-
Tibia	-	1	4	1	-	-	-
Talus	2	-	1	-	-	-	-
Calcaneus	1	-	-	-	-	-	-
Metatarsal	1	1	-	1	-	-	-
Proximal phalanx	-	-	1	-	-	-	-
NISP totals	*36*	*11*	*27*	*9*	*4*	*2*	*1*
Total weight	*1881*	*208*	*249.5*	*133*	*265*	*9*	*0.25*
MNI	*7*	*2*	*5*	*2*	*2*	*1*	*1*
% by NISP	*40*	*12*	*30*	*10*	*4*	*2*	*1*
% by weight	*69*	*8*	*9*	*4.8*	*9.6*	*0.3*	*0.01*

mandibles which were recorded according to Grant's system show a range of ages. There are more adults than juveniles, and in a larger sample this may be used to argue for the importance of wool, as at Porchester Castle, Hampshire, during the Saxon period (Grant 1982, 106). The sample size at Henbury is too small, however, for the suggestion to carry any weight.

Animal bone assemblages of comparable date from the Bristol area are in short supply. The animal bone from a small Mid-Late Iron Age settlement at Cribbs Causeway shows several similarities with the Henbury assemblage, although it appears to be slightly earlier in date (Maltby 1998). The extremely fragmentary nature of the material is notable in both assemblages. At Cribbs Causeway 75% of the animal bone could not be identified to species. Sheep were the most numerous taxa there, and at Henbury when sheep and sheep/goat are considered together these also outnumber cattle. The preservation of jaws and teeth at Cribbs Causeway was very poor so there is no tooth wear data for comparison with the Henbury sheep. Pig, horse and dog were also present in small quantities at Cribbs Causeway.

A much larger assemblage of slightly earlier date was recovered from Hallen (Hamilton-Dyer 2002) totalling over 5000 fragments. Problems of fragmentation were not as severe as at Cribbs Causeway, and 40% of bones could be identified to taxon. The same pattern found at Henbury and Cribbs Causeway is represented in the large assemblage at Hallen, with sheep being the most numerous domesticate followed by cattle, and much smaller quantities of horse, pig and dog. The fact that pig is quite poorly represented in all three assemblages is the normal situation for Iron Age sites in southern England (Maltby 1981). A small quantity of very young lamb bones was identified at Hallen but no neonatal specimens were found (Hamilton-Dyer 2002, 7).

Table 9: Animal bone: summary of assessment results for Periods 2 and 3

Species: E = Equus caballus (Horse), B = Bos taurus (cow), O/C = Ovis/Capra (sheep/goat), S = Sus scrofa (pig), D = Canis familiaris (dog), MUS = Mus sp (mouse), CH = Gallus (Chicken), CSZ = cow-sized, SSZ = sheep-sized, CHSZ = chicken-sized, PGSZ = pigeon-sized, UNID = unidentified.
Parts: H = head, HC = horncore, V = vertebra, R = rib, UL = upper limb, LL = lower limb, MP = metapodial, P = phalange, LB = long bone, F = fragment.
State: WE = weathered, BT = butchery marks, BN = burnt, GN = gnawed, RT = root etching, MB = modern break.
Age: I = infant, J = juvenile, SA = sub-adult, A = adult, O = old adult.

Feature type	No. fragments	No. bones	Weight (g)	No. bones identifiable to species	mandibles	No. epiphyses	species/parts	State	Age
Period 2									
Ditches and gullies	359	337	3149	75	9	18	E (H,LL,MP,P) B (H,UL,LL,MP,P) O/C (H,UL,LL, MP) S (H, MP) CSZ (H,V,LL,LB,R) SSZ (R,V,UL,LL,LB) UNID(F)	WE, BT, MB, GN, RT, BN	A, SA, J, I
Pits and postholes	223	219	1106.5	28	-	10	B (H,UL,LL,MP) O/C (H, LL, MP, P) CSZ (UL, LL, LB, V, R) SSZ (LB,R) UNID(F)	BT, MB, WE	A
Layers	64	63	340	23	-	4	B (H,UL,MP) O/C (H,MP,P) S (H,UL) MUS (H,LL)CSZ (V,LB) SSZ (LB) UNID(F)	BT, GN, BN, WE	A, SA
Period 3									
Ditches and gullies	501	480	3667	75	3	14	E(H,MP) B(H,UL,LL,MP) O/C(H,MP) S(H,UL) CSZ(H,V,LL,LB) SSZ(H,V,LL,LB) UNID(LB,F)	BT WE GN MB RT BN	A, SA
Pits	342	325	1520	43	-	5	E(H,UL,LL) B(H,UL,LL,P) S(H) O/C(H,V,UL,MP) D(H) CH(V,LL) CSZ(H,LB,R) SSZ(UL,R,LB,MP) CHSZ(LB) UNID(F)	BT, MB, GN, BN, WE	A, SA, I, O
Layers	694	678	5251	145	9	23	E(H,P) B(H,HC,UL,LL,MP) O/C(H,UL,LL,MP,P) S(H,UL,LL,P) D(H) PGSZ(UL) CSZ(V,R,UL,LL,LB) SSZ(V,LL,LB,MP)UNID(F)	BT WE MB GN BN	A, SA, O
Graves	116	116	76	9	-	-	E(H) O/C(H) S(H) CSZ(LL,LB) SSZ(LB,R) UNID(F)	WE BN MB	A

The small assemblage from Period 1 at Marshfield (Morgan 1985), to the north-east of Bristol, is of comparable date to Period 1 at Henbury, and with only 59 identifiable fragments it is also of comparable size. A very similar set of species was identified, although horse was not present until the Roman period and wild deer and hare contrast with the entirely domestic species found at Henbury. The large well-preserved animal assemblage from Frocester (Noddle 2000) is also useful for comparison, with a substantial quantity of material dating to before the end of the 1st century AD. Cattle are most numerous by fragment count, whilst sheep have the highest MNI values. Combined with the small proportions of pig, horse and dog the composition of the Frocester assemblage matches that of Henbury.

The animal bone from Henbury shows many similarities with those from nearby sites of mid-late Iron Age date. While Period 1 extends into the second half of the 1st century AD, there is nothing to suggest any changes in the choice of domestic species that are commonly attributed to the adoption of 'Roman' agricultural practices. A greater number of well-dated early Roman assemblages are required to understand the transition or adaptation of the agricultural system and economy during the period spanning the 1st and 2nd centuries AD in the Bristol region. The agricultural economy of Henbury during the 1st century AD, based on the limited data available, was of mixed farming focusing on cattle and ovicaprids with the cultivation of emmer/spelt and possibly wild grasses for fodder (see *charred plant remains*, below).

Charred plant remains, by Wendy Carruthers

Charred plant remains were recovered from nine samples in total: six flots and three residues. These were assessed (CA 2005). The potential for charred plant remains from Period 1 samples was deemed to be poor, and given the difficulties of interpretation in Periods 2 and 3 no further work was recommended on the charred plant remains recovered from these features. A summary of the assessment results is presented below. Further details including sample processing methods can be found in the site archive.

Small quantities of cereal remains were recovered from two samples from Period 1 features: the fill of pit 129 (sample <2>) and the primary fill of Ditch 1 (sample <7>). These consist of grains of emmer/spelt and bread wheat as well as chaff and wild grains. Useful quantities of charred plant remains were observed in flots recovered from Period 2 occupation deposit 057 (sample <9>) and the infills of Period 2 Ditch 14 (samples <2001> and <2002>) and Period 3 Ditch 15 (sample <8>). Samples <8> and <9> contained larger quantities of cereal grains, which may be derived from burnt spikelets that had been accidentally charred during parching, rather than pure cereal processing waste (chaff and weed seeds). Samples <2001> and <2002> were richer in chaff and resembled the waste product from a processing stage where parched spikelets were being broken up to remove the grain (Hillman 1981). Processing waste (chaff and weed seeds) may have been a useful resource, since it burns rapidly, can be fed to livestock, and can be mixed with clay and used as a building material. It was often used to fuel ovens and kilns (Van der Veen 1989). The cereal sprouts present in samples <2001> and <2002> may indicate malting but are more likely to reflect grain production and storage on a large scale, resulting in some spoilage due to sprouting. The recovery of larger quantities of charred cereal remains from later Roman samples is a common occurrence as large-scale cultivation and processing of spelt wheat increased during the Later Roman period.

DISCUSSION
by Neil Holbrook

The excavations at Henbury have provided valuable new evidence for the nature of Later Iron Age and Roman occupation in the Bristol region. The opportunity to examine a Late Iron Age farmstead is particularly welcome as previous work in the area has concentrated on the better known hillforts of Kings Weston and Blaise Castle. Henbury can also be usefully compared and contrasted with the Mid-Late Iron Age settlements examined at Hallen and Northwick (some 6km north-east of Hallen) on the Avonmouth Levels (Fig. 1). Interpretation of the Henbury evidence is, however, not straightforward. The ground levelling in 1982, while leading to the identification of the site, appears to have removed many shallowly dug features within Enclosure 1, hindering understanding of its internal layout and function. The later Roman activity was clearly intensive, but differential preservation combined with the restricted extent of Areas B and C make this difficult to understand.

A total of 24 crouched inhumation burials was discovered in 1982 and 2004. It is likely that an unknown number of further burials was destroyed in 1982 before BAARG became aware of the site. That the cemetery is earlier than Enclosure 1 is clear, as burials SK2 and SK21 were cut by the enclosure ditch, while SK1, SK19 and SK20 lay in a position that would have been occupied by an internal bank. It is conceivable that the burials lay some distance from a contemporary settlement within an unexcavated part of the site, or alternatively that all trace of unenclosed activity that preceded Enclosure 1 has not survived the ground levelling. Males and females were almost equally represented amongst the skeletons subjected to osteological analysis, while there was only a single child. The burials occur within a discrete part of the site but no boundaries which delimited the cemetery survived. The predominant north/south orientation and the lack of intercutting amongst the graves suggest that they were marked at ground level by mounds or some other means. In this context we should also note that the grave of SK4 might have been marked by a four-post structure of some description. A variety of timber mortuary and ritual structures have been found in association with a Late Iron Cremation Cemetery at Westhampnett, West Sussex (Fitzpatrick 1997, 32–5, 234), and indeed some four-post structures have been suggested as scaffolds for displaying corpses, among other interpretations (Ellison and Drewett 1971, 190–2). Sadly we cannot demonstrate conclusively that the timber structure is contemporary with the grave, and one of its postholes cut SK5. Therefore it remains entirely possible that the structure is later and was constructed without reference or even knowledge of the earlier burial. While no obvious patterning in the distribution of the burials is apparent, it is possible that the two examples of intercutting burials (SK2/3 and SK19/20) might be significant. In both cases the burials comprise a male and ?female and so it is tempting to regard the later burials as having family/kin associations with the primary inhumation. Adjacent burials SK4 and SK5 might be another example of this pairing. Nowakowski (1991, 210–32) suggested that it might be possible to discern family groupings within the later Iron Age inhumation cemetery at Trethellan, Cornwall.

Unfortunately the burials remain poorly dated despite the attempts to obtain radiocarbon determinations. A scrap of pottery contained within the backfill of SK16 produced a radiocarbon date in the Late Bronze Age (see *the radiocarbon dates*, above), but the sole grave good, a copper-alloy finger ring from SK9, is Middle or Late Iron Age. While Late

Bronze Age crouched inhumations are by no means unknown, to take the evidence on face value suggests that burial spanned a minimum of four centuries. This seems unlikely and it is simplest to consider that the potsherd was a residual component of the grave fill and ascribe all the burials to the Mid-Late Iron Age. Further precision is not possible. There are a few features which have yielded a small quantity of pottery that is more likely to be Middle Iron Age (*c.* 4th-1st century BC) than the bulk of the wares associated with Enclosure 1, which probably date exclusively to the 1st century AD. It is possible that the cemetery is contemporary with this activity.

The Henbury cemetery joins a growing body of evidence for crouched inhumation in the later Iron Age in the Cotswold-Severn region. Such burials are found predominantly in pits or scattered within or beyond settlements (Moore 2006, 69–71). The tradition continued throughout the 1st century AD and well into the 2nd century (Holbrook 2003, 65–6). What is particularly notable about Henbury is that rather than scattered burials we have good evidence here for a cemetery. Later Iron Age and early Roman rural inhumation cemeteries are a rarity in western Britain. At Yarnton, Oxfordshire, a cemetery containing 25 inhumations has been dated to the 4th-3rd century BC by radiocarbon dating (Hey *et al.* 1999), while at Sudden Farm, Hampshire, an Early-Mid Iron Age cemetery of in excess of 30 crouched inhumations was dug into an abandoned quarry just outside a settlement enclosure. Perhaps the closest parallels to Henbury are to be found in the inhumation cemeteries of west Devon and Cornwall (Whimster 1981, 1923). Here burials were normally placed in cist graves, but at Trethellan a small cemetery of 21 individuals placed in simple graves has been excavated (Nowakowski 1991, 210–32). It probably dates to the 2nd/1st century BC–1st century AD. Grave goods were few (like Henbury), eight bodies being buried with simple brooches and rings. Given the evidence for trade links along the Bristol Channel in the later Iron Age it may not be entirely fanciful to suggest that knowledge of the cemeteries on the north coast of the south-west peninsula could have permeated as far afield as Henbury. Equally it is highly unlikely that Henbury sits in isolation and similar cemeteries doubtless await discovery in the Cotswold-Severn region. Indeed Cunliffe (2005, 552) considers that Iron Age inhumation cemeteries could have been quite widespread, the current lack of examples being attributable to the dearth of excavation that has taken place around the periphery of settlements. A similar situation pertains in the early Roman period when rural cemeteries continue to be rare, a notable exception being Hucclecote near Gloucester which contained predominately crouched inhumations and dated to the first half of the 2nd century AD (Thomas *et al.* 2003).

Enclosure 1 appears to date to the early 1st century AD. While later than the cemetery the enclosure appears to have been sited to largely exclude the burials from its interior. This suggests that the cemetery was still regarded with reverence by the enclosure builders, which in turn favours continuity of occupation during Period 1 and probably only a short time gap between the cessation of burial and the commencement of construction of the enclosure. The enclosure was rectangular in shape, with no ditch dug to define its north-west side. This was the wettest part of the site, and it is conceivable that the high water table led the builders to define this side of the enclosure with a fence or hedge rather than a ditch, all trace of which has been destroyed by a combination of ground levelling and the later digging of Ditch 8 of Enclosure 2. Rectilinear enclosures defined on only three sides by ditches are, however, unusual (Moore 2006, fig. 4.6). There was seemingly no entrance on the north-east and south-east sides, but two to the south-west. These provided access into a partially enclosed annex or close bounded to the east by Ditches 2 and 3 while the south side probably lay beyond the excavation area. Enclosure 1 (*c.* 85m long by 50m wide) is comparable in size with the Late Iron Age (Period 2.3b) farmstead at Frocester Court (73m x 40m) which also had partially ditched closes attached to one side of the enclosure (Price 2000, 173–8). The principal difficulty in the interpretation of Enclosure 1 is the absence of internal features. It is probable that this is a consequence of ground levelling having destroyed all trace of insubstantial features such as turf or cob-built roundhouses (which are known elsewhere in the Severn Vale and frequently leave little archaeological trace). Deep storage pits commonly found on Iron Age sites in Wessex are much less common in this region, the pits inside the enclosure at Frocester Court being fairly shallow (ibid., 173–8). The high water table at Henbury would also have rendered deep pits of little value for storage. Ground truncation could therefore have quite easily removed all internal features. An alternative explanation is that such features never existed, and that the enclosure was not a settlement but rather a stock corral. If this was the case, however, it is difficult to understand why the builders went to the effort of digging a rock-cut ditch when a lesser barrier would have sufficed. A further possibility, which would also account for the absence of a ditch on the north-west side, is that construction was abandoned before Enclosure 1 was completed. Against this suggestion is the apparent evidence for recutting of the enclosure ditch recorded in two locations, and the accumulation of silt in the base of the ditch before the bank was levelled. It is difficult to be firm on the interpretation of Enclosure 1 but on balance interpretation as a farmstead which has suffered truncation is preferred.

The farmstead at Henbury adds to our understanding of the Iron Age settlement pattern of north-west Bristol (Fig. 1). It lies less than 1km from the hillfort at Blaise Castle which was occupied in the later Iron Age and conceivably throughout much of the Roman period as well (Rahtz and Clevedon Brown 1959). Another farmstead has been examined at Cribbs Causeway, Filton, where a small enclosure containing a single roundhouse appears to have been set within a field system (FA 1998). Residual Iron Age pottery has also been recovered from Lawrence Weston (Boore 2000). The relationship between farmsteads like Henbury with the still poorly known settlements on the Avonmouth Levels is a matter of interest. The best examined are those at Hallen and Northwick. Hallen appears to date to the 2nd–1st century BC and is interpreted as a short-lived, possibly seasonal settlement associated with the grazing of livestock on the marshes. A series of ditches at Northwick date to the 1st century AD and are interpreted as paddocks for seasonal grazing (Gardiner *et al.* 2002). No evidence for cereal cultivation was recovered from either site. The small environmental assemblage from the Period 1 features at Henbury is consistent with a mixed farm that reared cattle and sheep and cultivated cereals. Perhaps stock was taken from farms such as Henbury and Cribbs Causeway onto the drier parts of the Avonmouth Levels in the summer to feed off the lush grasslands? Settlements like Hallen may have been little more than the summer homes of a small number of shepherds and stockmen. This would suggest a well-developed and integrated agricultural economy in the area that successfully exploited the differing environmental zones, with Blaise Castle performing an important role in the articulation of trade networks. We cannot be certain on current evidence, however, that the hillfort was still in use in the 1st century AD when Enclosure 1 was built.

To judge from the pottery within the ditch fills of Enclosure 1 the bank of the enclosure was partially slighted into the ditch at some date between *c.* AD 50 and AD 100, and quite possibly earlier rather than later in that range. The denuded bank and ditch remained sufficiently visible landscape features to determine the location and orientation of Enclosure 2 and the activity bounded by Ditch 7 in the south-east part of the site. It is conceivable that Enclosure 1 served some agricultural purpose at this time. Occupation within Enclosure 2 dates to the 2nd and 3rd century AD, and there is no evidence or suggestion in the pottery for any break in occupation. At this time Henbury probably comprised a complex of settlement enclosures, paddocks and field systems typical of many Romano-British rural settlements. Whether the abandonment of Enclosure 1 has any connection with the construction of the Roman road, which is likely to date to the decades following the establishment of the fortress at Kingsholm, Gloucester, in *c.* AD 49/50, is difficult to say, not least because it is not entirely assured that the road ran adjacent to the settlement. Some further support for the postulated alignment of the Roman road has recently come from an evaluation a short distance to the north of the present excavation area. Two trenches excavated across the road's anticipated line both revealed cobbled surfaces. While these surfaces were undated, Roman pottery was found in the vicinity (Payne 2006). More generally it is likely that the abandonment of Enclosure 1 was related to changes in the settlement pattern resulting from the establishment and development of a small town at Sea Mills, only 4km distant, in the second half of the 1st century AD. Little more can be said of the layout of the settlement in Period 2. Certainly there is no evidence at all to suggest that it developed into a roadside settlement such as occur widely throughout lowland Britain. There are no obvious buildings within the excavation area at this time, although it is conceivable that Ditches 15 and 20 might define the site of a rectangular timber structure up to 25m long and 10m wide. If so the ephemeral traces invite comparison with the some of the 2nd and 3rd-century AD buildings at Frocester Court (Price 2000).

The Period 3 activity was clearly intensive but once again recognition of buildings is difficult although there is good reason to believe that the spreads of stone found in the south-east corner of Area A and in Areas B and C served as foundation rafts for timber structures. That in Area A contained numerous fragments of Pennant sandstone roofing tile suggesting that it was formed from rubble from an earlier building. Rectangular spreads of stone have been identified at a number of other farmsteads in the Bristol region where, frequently in the absence of other evidence for structures, they have been suggested as foundation rafts for timber buildings which have otherwise left no trace. Examples can be cited from Cattybrook, Almondsbury (Bennett 1980, 167); Heneage Court, Falfield (Miles and Bennett 1974) and Filwood Park, Whitchurch (Williams 1983; Cox 1997). Dry-stone footings, with little or no foundations, which probably supported timber or cob superstructures have also been found at sites such as Baileys Court Farm, Stoke Gifford (Russell 1989). We can therefore reasonably infer that there were several timber structures present in Period 3 at Henbury.

The evidence such as we have it is consistent with continuous occupation from the Late Iron Age through to the very end of the 4th century AD. In some respects the sequence resembles that at Frocester Court, but whereas that farmstead was swept away for the construction of a villa *c.* AD 275, Henbury continued as an unpretentious farming settlement throughout the late Roman period. Henbury also adds to the ample evidence for the intensive Roman settlement of north-west Bristol (Russell and Williams 1984, fig. 2), and while the character of these sites is still poorly known, with the obvious exception of the Kingsweston villa (Boon 1950), the work reported here highlights the potential for future study.

ACKNOWLEDGEMENTS

The excavation and this publication were funded by HBG Construction Western Limited on behalf of Bristol City Council, Children and Young People's Services. We are grateful to Tim Buckley of HBG Construction Western Limited and Bob Jones of Bristol City Council for their assistance. The excavation was managed by Simon Cox and led by David Kenyon assisted by Franco Vartuca. Post-excavation analysis was undertaken by Richard Young and latterly Derek Evans. The post-excavation was managed by Annette Hancocks and the illustrations were prepared by Lorna Gray. The text was edited by Neil Holbrook and Annette Hancocks. We are extremely grateful to Dr Tom Moore for his comments and insights which have greatly improved the discussion of the Iron Age remains and to Bob Jones for his comments on the final report. Teresa Gilmore thanks Malin Holst for comments on an earlier draft of the human bone report. The project archives and finds will be deposited with Bristol's Museums, Galleries and Archives under accession numbers BRSMG 2003/9 and 2003.93.

BIBLIOGRAPHY

Allen, J.R.L. 1998 'Late Iron Age and Earliest Roman Calcite-tempered Ware from Sites on the Severn Estuary Levels: Character and Distribution', *Studia Celtica* **32**, 27–42

Anderson, A.S., Wacher, J.S. and Fitzpatrick, A.P. 2001 *The Romano-British 'Small Town' at Wanborough, Wiltshire* Britannia Monograph Series **19**, London, Society for the Promotion of Roman Studies

ApSimon, A.M. 1959 'Iron Age Pottery', in P. Rahtz and J. Clevedon Brown 1959, 160–4

BaRAS (Bristol and Region Archaeological Service) 2001 *Archaeological desktop study of Henbury School, Henbury, Bristol* unpublished BaRAS report no. **853/2001**

Barber, A., Cox, S. and Hancocks, A. (forthcoming) 'A Late Iron Age and Roman farmstead at RAF St Athan, Vale of Glamorgan: evaluation and excavation 2002–3' *Archaeol. Cambrensis*

Barford, P.M. 1985 'Objects of stone', in K. Blockley 1985, 240

Barrett, J.C., Freeman, P.W.M. and Woodward, A. 2000 *Cadbury Castle, Somerset: the later prehistoric and early historic archaeology* London, English Heritage

Bass, W.M. 1995 *Human Osteology: a Laboratory and Field Manual* Missouri, Missouri Archaeological Society

Bennett, J. 1980 'A Romano-British settlement at Cattybrook, Almondsbury, Avon', *CRAAGS Occ. Paper* **5**, Bristol, Committee for Rescue Archaeology in Avon, Gloucestershire and Somerset

Bennett, J. 1985 *Sea Mills: the Roman town of Abonae: excavations at Nazareth House, 1972* City of Bristol Museum and Art Gallery Monograph **3**, Bristol, City of Bristol Museum and Art Gallery

BGS (British Geological Survey) 1971 *1:50,000 Solid and Drift map sheet 264: Bristol*

Boon, G.C. 1950 'The Roman villa in Kingsweston Park (Lawrence Weston Estate) Gloucestershire', *Trans. Bristol Gloucestershire Archaeol. Soc.* **69**, 5–58

Boore, E. 2000 'A Romano-British site at Lawrence Weston, Bristol, 1995', *Bristol Avon Archaeol.* **16**, 1–47

Blockley, K. 1985 *Marshfield: Ironmongers Piece excavations 1982–3. An Iron Age and Romano-British settlement in the South Cotswolds* BAR British Series **141**, Oxford, British Archaeological Reports

Bronk Ramsey 2005 OxCal version 3.10

Brothwell, D.R. 1976 'Further evidence of bone chewing by ungulates: the sheep of North Ronaldsay, Orkney', *J. Archaeol. Sci.* **3**, 179–82

Brothwell, D.R. 1981 *Digging up bones* London, British Museum (Natural History)

Bryant, V. and Evans, J. 2004 'Iron Age and Romano-British pottery', in H. Dalwood and R. Edwards 2004, 240–80

Buikstra, J.E. and Ubelaker, D.H. (eds) 1994 *Standards for data collection in human skeletal remains* Arkansas, Arkansas Archaeological Survey Research Seminars **44**

Bulleid, A. and Gray, H.G. 1917 *The Glastonbury Lake Village ii, Glastonbury* Taunton, Glastonbury Antiquarian Society

Butcher, S.A. 2001 'Brooches of Copper Alloy', in A. Anderson *et al.* 2001, 41–69

CA (Cotswold Archaeology) 2003 *Henbury Secondary School, Marissal Road, Henbury, Bristol: Archaeological Evaluation* CA typescript report no. **03031**

CA (Cotswold Archaeology) 2004 *Henbury Secondary School, Marissal Road, Henbury, Bristol: Archaeological Evaluation (Phase 2) and Watching Brief* CA typescript report no. **04001**

CA (Cotswold Archaeology) 2005 *Henbury Secondary School, Bristol: Post-Excavation Assessment and Updated Project Design* CA typescript report no. **04200**

Clifford, E.M. 1961 *Bagendon: a Belgic Oppidum* Cambridge, Heffer and Sons

Collis, J. 1977 'Owslebury (Hants) and the problem of burials on rural settlements', in R. Reece (ed.) 1977, 26–34

Cox, S. 1997 'Further evidence of a Romano-British agricultural settlement at Filwood Park, Bristol, 1998', *Bristol Avon Archaeol.* **14**, 59–73

Crummy, N. 1979 'A chronology of Romano-British bone pins', *Britannia* **10**, 157–63

Cunliffe, B.W. 1975 *Excavations at Portchester Castle, Vol. 1: Roman* Reports of the Research Committee of the Society of Antiquaries of London **XXXII**, London, Society of Antiquaries

Cunliffe, B. 2005 *Iron Age Communities in Britain (4th edition)* Abingdon, Routledge

Dalwood, H. and Edwards, R. 2004 *Excavations at Deansway, Worcester 1988–89: Romano-British small town to medieval city* York, Council for British Archaeology

Dudley, D. 1968 'Excavations on Nor'nour in the Isles of Scilly, 1962–6', *Archaeol. J.* **124**, 1–64

Ellis, P. 1987 'Sea Mills, Bristol: the 1965–1968 excavations in the Roman town of Abonae', *Trans. Bristol Gloucestershire Archaeol. Soc.* **105**, 15–108

Ellison, A. and Drewett, P. 1971 'Pits and postholes in the British early Iron Age: some alternative explanations', *Proc. Prehist. Soc.* **37**, 183–94

FA (Foundations Archaeology) 1998 *Land at Cribbs Causeway, Filton: Archaeological Evaluation and Excavation* unpublished FA typescript report

Fitzpatrick, A. 1997 *Archaeological excavations on the route of the A27 Westhampnett bypass, West Sussex. Volume 2: the cemeteries.* Wessex Archaeology Report **12**, Salisbury, Trust for Wessex Archaeology

Fitzpatrick, A.P. 2004 'Roman Britain in 2003. 8. South-Western Counties', *Britannia* **35**, 303–9

Foster, J. 2000 'Copper alloy rings', in J.C. Barrett *et al.* 2000, 194

Fowler, P.J. and Bennett J. 1974 'Archaeology and the M5 Motorway. Third Report', *Trans. Bristol Gloucestershire Archaeol. Soc.* **93**, 101–30

Gardiner, J., Allen, J., Hamilton-Dyer, S., Laidlaw, M. and Scaife, R. 2002 'Making the most of it: later prehistoric pastoralism in the Avon Levels, Severn Estuary', *Proc. Prehist. Soc.* **68**, 1–39

GeoQuest Associates 2002 *Geophysical Survey of an area of proposed development at Henbury School, Marissal Road, Henbury, Bristol* unpublished typescript report

Gillam, J.P. 1976 'Coarse fumed ware in North Britain and beyond', *Glasgow Arch. J.* **4**, 57–80

Grant, A. 1975 'The use of tooth wear as a guide to the age of domestic animals', in B. Cunliffe 1975, 437–50

Grant, A. 1982 'The use of tooth wear as a guide to the age of domestic ungulates', in B. Wilson *et al.* 1982, 91–108

Hamilton-Dyer, S. 2002 'The animal bone assemblage' in J. Gardiner *et al.* 2002, 7–10

Hey, G., Bayliss, A. and Boyle, A. 1999 'Iron Age burials at Yarnton, Oxfordshire', *Antiquity* **73**, no. 281, 551–62

Hillman, G. 1981 'Reconstructing crop husbandry practices from charred remains of crops', in R. Mercer (ed.) 1981, 123–62

Holbrook, N. 2003 'Discussion', in A. Thomas *et al.* 2003, 62–7

Hooley, D. 2001 'Copper alloy and silver objects', in A. Anderson *et al.* 2001, 75–120

Hull, M.R. 1968 'The Nor'nour Brooches', in D. Dudley 1968, 28–64

Isaac, A. 2001 'Iron objects', in A. Anderson *et al.* 2001, 121–47

Jones, M. and Dimbleby, G. 1981 *The environment of man: the Iron-Age to the Anglo-Saxon period* BAR British Series **87**, Oxford, British Archaeological Reports

Laidlaw, M. 2002 'Appendix: pottery fabrics, forms and decoration', in J. Gardiner *et al.* 2002, 35–9

Leach P. with Evans, C.J. 2001 *Fosse Lane, Shepton Mallet 1990: Excavation of a Romano-British Roadside Settlement in Somerset,* Britannia Monograph Series **18**, London, Society for the Promotion of Roman Studies

Levitan, B. 1985 'The animal bone', in J. Bennett 1985, 56–8

Lovejoy, C.O., Meindl, R.S., Pryzbeck, T.R. and Mensforth, R.P. 1985 'Chronological metamorphosis of the auricular surface of the ilium, a new method for the determination of adult skeletal age at death', *Amer. J. Phys. Anthrop.* **68**, 15–28

Lyman, R.L. 1994 *Vertebrate Taphonomy* Cambridge, Cambridge University Press

MacGregor, A. 1985 *Bone, Antler, Ivory and Horn: the technology of skeletal materials since the Roman period* London, Croom Helm

Maltby, M. 1981 'Iron-Age, Romano-British and Anglo-Saxon animal husbandry; a review of the faunal evidence', in J. Jones and G. Dimbleby 1981, 155–204

Maltby, M. 1998 'Appendix 2: Animal Bone', in FA 1998

Manchester, K. and Roberts, C.A. 1995 *Archaeology of Disease* Stroud, Sutton Publishing

Manning, W.H. 1985 *Catalogue of the Romano-British Iron Tools, Fittings and Weapons in the British Museum* London, British Museum Publications

Manning, W.H. 1993 *Report on the excavations at Usk 1965–1976: the Roman pottery* Cardiff, University of Cardiff Press

Margary, I.D. 1973 *Roman Roads in Britain (3rd edition)* London, John Baker

Mercer, R. (ed.) 1981 *Farming Practice in British Prehistory* Edinburgh, Edinburgh University Press

Miles, D. and Bennett, J. 1974 'Falfield, Heneage Court', in P. Fowler and J. Bennett 1974, 104–23

Moore, T. 2006 *Iron Age societies in the Severn-Cotswolds: developing narratives of social and landscape change* BAR British Series **421**, Oxford, British Archaeological Reports

Morgan, N.T. 1985 'Animal bones', in K. Blockley 1985, 330–52

Noddle, B. 2000 'Chapter 15: large vertebrate remains', in E. Price 2000, 217–43

Nowakowski, J. 1991 'Trethellan Farm, Newquay: excavation of a lowland Bronze Age settlement and Iron Age cemetery', *Cornish Archaeol.* **30**, 5–242

Payne, S. 1985 'Morphological distinctions between mandibular teeth of young sheep *Ovis* and goats *Capra*', *J. Archaeol. Sci.* **12**, 139–47

Payne, R. 2006 *Site off Marissal Road, Henbury, Bristol: archaeological evaluation project* Avon Archaeological Unit unpublished report

Peacock, D.P.S. 1969 'A contribution to the study of Glastonbury coarse ware from southwestern Britain', *Antiq. J.* **49**, 41–61

Price, E. 2000 *Frocester A Romano-British settlement, its antecedents and successors. Volume 2: The Finds* Stonehouse, Gloucester and District Archaeological Research Group

Prummel, W. 1987 'Atlas for identification of foetal skeletal elements of cattle, horse, sheep and pig. Part 2', *Archaeozoologia* **I** (2), 11–42

Rahtz, P.A. and Clevedon Brown, J. 1959 'Blaise Castle Hill, Bristol, 1957', *Trans. Bristol Univ. Speleol. Soc.* **8**, 147–71

Reece, R. (ed.) 1977 *Burial in the Roman World* CBA Research Report **22**, London, Council for British Archaeology

Rigby, V. 1982. 'The Coarse Pottery', in J. Wacher and A. McWhirr 1982, 153–204

Roberts, C.A. and Cox, M. 2003 *Health and Disease in Britain from Prehistory to the Present Day* Stroud, Sutton Publishing

Russell, J. 1983 'Romano-British Burials at Henbury Comprehensive School, Bristol: a preliminary report', *Bristol Avon Archaeol.* **2**, 21–4

Russell, J. 1989 'Excavations at Baileys Court Farm, Stoke Gifford, 1990 (a preliminary note)', *Bristol Avon Archaeol.* **8**, 53–4

Russell, J.R. and Williams, R.G.J. 1984 'Romano-British sites in the city of Bristol: a review and gazetteer', *Bristol Avon Archaeol.* **3**, 18–26

Sabin, J. 2000 'The Roman Coarseware Pottery', in E. Boore 2000, 37–44

Schmid, E. 1972 *Atlas of Animal Bones* Amsterdam and London, Elsevier

Schwartz, J.H. 1995 *Skeleton Keys* Oxford, Oxford University Press

Seyer, S. 1821 *Memoirs historical and topographical of Bristol and its neighbourhood, Volume 1* Bristol, Norton

Smith, A.F. 2003 *Henbury School, Marissal Road, Bristol: archaeological desktop study* Bristol Sites and Monuments Record no. **21375**

Stead, I.M. 1991 *Iron Age Cemeteries in East Yorkshire* London, English Heritage

Stuiver, M. and Polach, H.A. 1977 'Discussion: reporting of 14C data', *Radiocarbon* **19**, 355–63

Stuiver, M. and Reimer, P.J. 1993 'Extended 14C database and revised CALIB 3.0 14C Age calibration program', *Radiocarbon* **35** (1), 215–30

Stuiver, M., Reimer, P.J., Bard, E., Beck, J.W., Burr, G.S., Hughen, K.A., Kromer, B., McCormac, van der Plicht, J. and Spurk, M. 1998 'INTCAL98 Radiocarbon Age Calibration, 24000-0 cal. BP', *Radiocarbon* **40** (3), 1041–83

Thomas, A., Holbrook, N. and Bateman, C. 2003 *Late prehistoric and Romano-British burial and settlement at Hucclecote, Gloucestershire* Bristol and Gloucestershire Archaeol. Rep. 2, Cirencester, Cotswold Archaeology

Timby, J. 1987 'Other Roman Pottery', in P. Ellis 1987, 77–92

Timby J. 1998 'Pottery', in FA 1998

Tomber, R. and Dore, J. 1998 *The National Roman Fabric Reference Collection: a handbook* London, Museum of London Archaeology Service

University of Waikato Radiocarbon Dating Laboratory 2006 'Operating Procedures', www.radiocarbondating.com (viewed on 21.12.06)

Van Beek, G. 1983 *Dental morphology. An illustrated guide* Bristol, Wright

Van der Veen, M. 1989 'Charred grain assemblages from Roman-period corn driers in Britain', *Arch. J.* **146**, 302–19

Wacher, J. and McWhirr, A. 1982 *Early Roman Occupation at Cirencester* Cirencester Excavations **I**, Cirencester, Cirencester Excavation Committee

Webster, P.V., Gwilt, A. and Horák, J. (forthcoming) 'The pre-Roman pottery', in A. Barber *et al.* (forthcoming)

Wedlake, W.J. 1982 *The Excavation of the Shrine of Apollo at Nettleton, Wiltshire* London, Society of Antiquaries of London

Whimster, R. 1981 *Burial practices in Iron Age Britain* BAR British Series **90**, Oxford, British Archaeological Reports

Wilkins, H.J. 1920 *The Perambulation of the Boundaries of the Ancient Parish of Westbury-on-Trym in May 1803 AD* Bristol, Arrowsmith

Williams, R.J.G. 1983 'Romano-British settlement at Filwood Park, Bristol', *Bristol Avon Archaeol.* **2**, 12–19

Wilson, B., Grigson, C. and Payne, S. 1982 *Ageing and Sexing Animal bones from archaeological sites* BAR British Series **109**, Oxford, British Archaeological Reports

Young, C.J. 1977 *Oxfordshire Roman Pottery* BAR British Series **43**, Oxford, British Archaeological Reports

A POST-ROMAN CEMETERY AT HEWLETT PACKARD, FILTON, SOUTH GLOUCESTERSHIRE: EXCAVATIONS IN 2005

by Kate Cullen, Neil Holbrook, Martin Watts, Anwen Caffell and Malin Holst

with contributions by
Rowena Gale and Sylvia Warman

INTRODUCTION
by Kate Cullen and Martin Watts

During March and April 2005 Cotswold Archaeology (CA) carried out an archaeological excavation at Hewlett Packard, Filton, South Gloucestershire (centred on NGR: ST 6131 7784; Fig. 1). This work was undertaken at the request of Atisreal, on behalf of Hewlett Packard, in accordance with a condition attached to planning permission granted by South Gloucestershire Council for residential development of the site. The development area, which extends to some 30 hectares, lies partly within South Gloucestershire and partly within the City of Bristol. The excavation area, which was approximately 0.7 hectares, was near to the centre of the overall development site and entirely within the parish of Stoke Gifford in South Gloucestershire.

Topography and geology

Prior to redevelopment the site comprised largely uncultivated agricultural land within a local landscape of low relief, but one surrounded by extensive modern development (Fig. 2): to the west, Lockleaze School and playing fields; to the north, the Ministry of Defence Abbey Wood complex; to the north-east, Hewlett Packard; to the east, the Frenchay campus of the University of the West of England (UWE); and to the south-east, a modern housing development on the site of the former Stoke Park Hospital. The only exception was to the south, where the site was immediately adjacent to the Grade II Listed Stoke Park (see below). The excavation area was situated on a gentle north-west facing slope, falling from approximately 79m above OD in the south to 74m above OD in the north.

The solid geology of the area is mapped as being varied, with bands (from west to east) of clay, white and blue Lias limestone, clay and shale, and Keuper Marl (BGS 1971). During excavation the natural substrate was also found to vary, mostly comprising limestone brash but giving way to clays to the north and south.

Archaeological background

A desk-based assessment (CA 2003) concluded that no known archaeological sites lay within or immediately adjacent to the area of proposed development, but that evidence for possible prehistoric, Roman and medieval settlement was known from the vicinity, with more certain evidence of post-medieval activity.

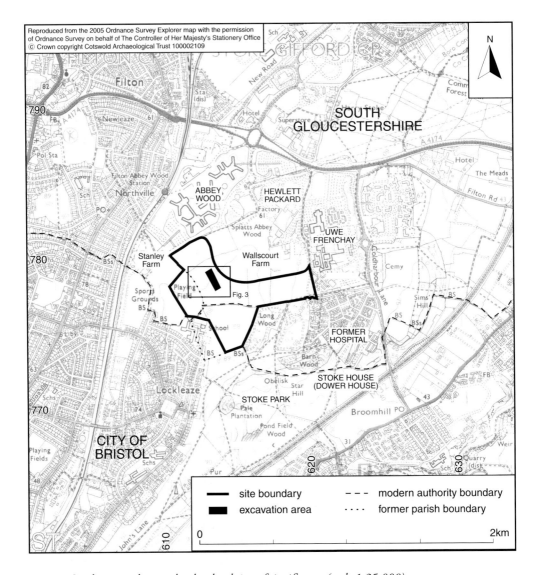

Fig. 1: Site location plan, with other local sites of significance (scale 1:25,000)

At the former Stoke Park Hospital (Fig.1), possible Iron Age field boundaries, kilns and a hearth were uncovered during an archaeological evaluation (Wessex Archaeology 1999). Ditches containing Roman pottery and the stone foundations of a rectangular structure were uncovered during excavation in advance of quarrying in the vicinity of Stoke House (Jancar 1981), and a small quantity of Roman pottery was retrieved during evaluation prior to the construction of the Abbey Wood complex (RPS Clouston 1992).

Until the 2005 investigations there was no recorded evidence of post-Roman or Saxon activity in the vicinity of the site. In the medieval period it lay within the manor and parish of Stoke Gifford. Strip lynchets preserved as earthworks within Stoke Park testify

Fig. 2:   Aerial view of the site, looking north-west

to medieval agriculture (Russell 1989, 32–4) while Wallscourt Farm to the north-east is first documented in the early 15th century (ibid., 30) and Stanley Farm to the west in 1276 (in the *Rotuli Hundredorum*). In the late 16th century the manor house of Stoke Gifford was moved from a site close to St Michael's church in Great Stoke to a new location at the southern end of the parish on the site now occupied by Stoke House (Russell 1989, 31). In 1738 Norborne Berkeley succeeded to the Stoke Gifford estate and in partnership with Thomas Wright set out upon the wholesale transformation of the woods and fields around the Elizabethan mansion into a landscaped park which still contains numerous 18th-century and later garden landscape features. The Grade II* Listed Stoke House (also known as Dower House) was built between 1749 and 1764 but retains elements of the original 16th-century house (Russell 1989, 35–40). The earliest known cartographic source to depict the site is a plan of 1725 entitled 'A map of Stoke Gifford, the seat of John Berkeley' (GRO photocopy 258), which shows that the site included a number of field boundaries that no longer survive, and provides the names of the then extant fields, many of which have since been amalgamated into larger plots.

Following assessment an archaeological evaluation was carried out, with 39 trenches excavated across the proposed development area (CA 2005). The only recognisably archaeological remains that appeared to pre-date the post-medieval period were at least seven undated human inhumation burials towards the northern end of trench 12 (Fig. 3). The burials were partly exposed to confirm their nature, but were not excavated at that stage. Remains of several boundary ditches and plough furrows were recorded in other trenches, including a flat-bottomed 1.5m-wide ditch that ran across trenches 11, 12,

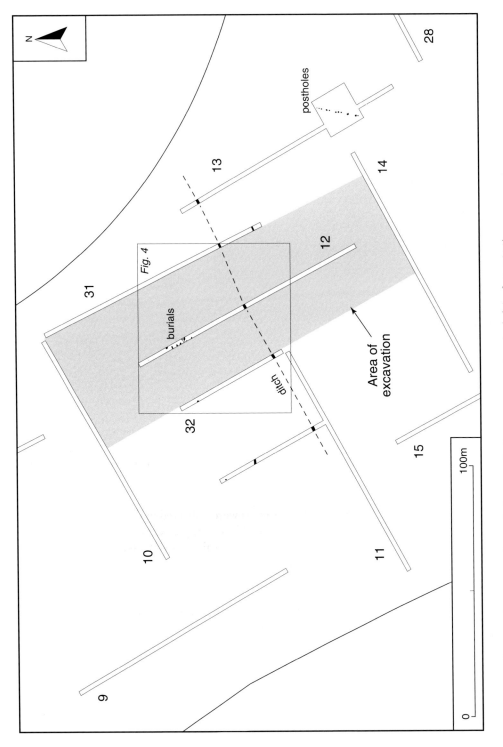

Fig. 3: Significant evaluation trenches with the area of subsequent excavation shaded (scale 1:1500)

13, 31 and 32 from north-east to south-west (Fig. 3). This ditch, which contained post-medieval pottery, was the remains of the boundary between two fields recorded in 1725 as 'Upper Locky' to the north and 'Little Lockly' to the south. By 1842 the boundary had been removed to create a larger field called 'Ha Ha Ground', a name possibly indicative of a deer park feature. The southern end of trench 13 was expanded to record a line of undated stone-packed postholes that continued beyond both limits of excavation (Fig. 3). This alignment did not relate to any recorded field boundaries but was thought to be of probable post-medieval or modern date (CA 2005, 9).

Methodology

The presence of an undated cemetery warranted full excavation prior to development in the vicinity of evaluation trench 12, which was carried out in accordance with a specification agreed with Mr David Haigh (Archaeology and Conservation Officer, South Gloucestershire Council). It was agreed that if no burials (or other significant features) were encountered within 15m of the surrounding evaluation trenches, that these could form the limits of excavation. Excavation revealed no significant features in proximity to the evaluation trenches, which therefore became the limits of excavation. The overall excavation area measured 145m by 50m (Fig. 3).

Work commenced with the mechanical removal of an average of 0.22m of topsoil and overburden, under archaeological supervision, to expose features cut into the underlying natural substrate. Many features were clearly defined immediately but others became visible only after a period of weathering had occurred. Features exposed included graves, tree-throw pits, other pits or possible postholes, a quarry pit, and a ditch with associated postholes. All features recorded in trench 12 during the evaluation were re-exposed and fully investigated during the main excavation. All graves were scanned by metal detector prior to excavation to identify any surviving metal artefacts such as coffin nails, although none were located.

All burials were fully excavated in accordance with guidelines prepared by the Institute of Field Archaeologists (McKinley and Roberts 1993) with every skeleton recorded in plan by digital, colour slide, and black-and-white photography. Due to the highly fragmentary nature of the human remains and the difficulty in identifying bone within the heavy clay fills of the graves, the basal contents of the graves were collected in their entirety following excavation of the visible parts of each skeleton. These samples were then dried and sorted by hand to increase the recovery of human bone. In this report all skeletons are referred to by their skeleton number, prefixed SK.

Artefactual material was scarce and not enough was recovered to date the cemetery with any confidence, therefore a programme of radiocarbon dating using human bone was undertaken, once specialist analysis had been completed. Date ranges cited in the text are those at 95.4% confidence level (2 sigma) unless otherwise specified.

EXCAVATION RESULTS
by Kate Cullen and Martin Watts

The excavation revealed the surviving remains of the cemetery to comprise 51 graves within an area of approximately 20m by 10m, with a number of other features in the northern part of the excavation area (Fig. 4). The most obvious of these was the post-medieval ditch to the south of the cemetery, as identified during the evaluation, which bisected the excavation area (Figs 3 and 4). The ditch was accompanied by a parallel alignment of 16 postholes. Also dating to the post-medieval period was a large subrectangular pit, measuring 3.5m by 1.2m and 0.35m in depth, just to the east of the cemetery (Fig. 3). It contained redeposited natural substrate and outcropping bedrock was exposed at its base, suggesting this had once been a quarry pit. Other features included undated tree-throw pits and other pits or possible postholes, all to the north of the post-medieval ditch (see below).

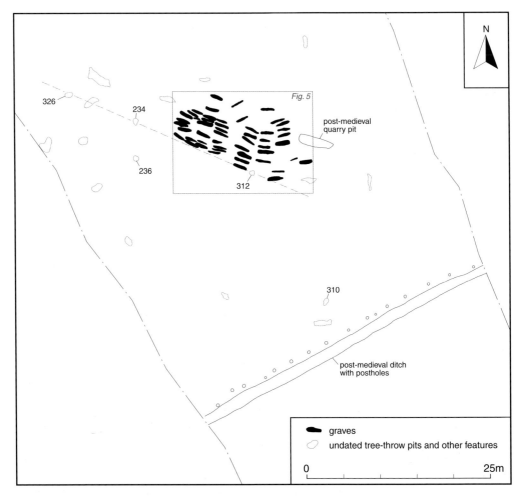

Fig. 4: Plan of all excavated features (scale 1:500)

The post-Roman cemetery (Figs 5 and 6)

The 51 graves were arranged in groups of discrete and generally compact rows within the cemetery. All the graves were aligned broadly east/west, although there was some variation between groups, and almost all graves were filled with redeposited natural brash comprising yellowish or reddish brown silty clay with limestone fragments, which made the identification of some graves difficult. Overall there was very little intercutting between graves. All had rounded ends but varied considerably in length (between 0.88m and 2.45m) and width (between 0.37m to 0.75m). The survival of some graves to only 0.04m in depth was indicative of the high degree of post-depositional truncation and disturbance of the cemetery, almost certainly through ploughing, which had contributed to the variation of surviving dimensions in plan. Overall, only half survived to more than 0.2m in depth, and the deepest grave was less than 0.5m deep.

The graves all contained single inhumation burials with the heads to the west, except for one burial that had been disturbed. All bar one of the undisturbed burials were supine (face up). Post-depositional disturbance to the graves had affected many of the skeletons within: several bone fragments were retrieved from the topsoil during stripping, and it was clear that numerous bones within graves been disturbed by ploughing activity. In general, bone survival was poor, particularly in the shallower graves, and no skeleton was more than 80% complete (see *the human bone*, below).

No grave goods were present and very few other finds were recorded. Only six graves contained small, abraded sherds of Roman or Late Iron Age pottery. Four radiocarbon determinations date the cemetery to the 5th to 7th centuries AD, indicating that this pottery is residual. No coffin nails or any other evidence for coffins were recovered, and the majority of skeletons fitted tightly within the graves. Just over half of the graves contained one or two fragments of animal bone, which like the pottery is all believed to be a residual, incidental component of the grave fills. The presence of additional human bone from the disturbance of earlier graves was noted only occasionally, with one possible case of a female buried with a foetus or neonate.

Nine groups of graves have been identified from their spatial distribution, and are described below. Arm positions were noted but formed no obvious pattern, and osteological analysis has not identified any divisions or patterns based on sex or age-at-death (see *discussion*), although the poor bone survival and incompleteness of the skeletons affected identification of all of these attributes. The results are summarised in Table 1.

Group 1 comprised a pair of parallel graves (102, 105), both orientated north-east/south-west lying 1.75m apart in the central-northern part of the cemetery. Both graves were shallow and contained poorly preserved adult female skeletons. SK104, within grave 102, produced a radiocarbon date of 410–560 cal. AD (Wk-17498).

Group 2 was the largest, comprising 25 burials within a broadly rectangular area measuring 8m by 5m at the western end of the cemetery. All of the graves were orientated north-west/south-east. Most of the graves were aligned in rows, albeit poorly defined ones towards the west. There was some clustering of graves within the rows, particularly to the north. The overall impression was of a group of burials surrounding, but at a short distance from, a central grave (180). This impression was reinforced by a number of the surrounding graves intercutting, which was only apparent in this group.

As well as being the apparent focus of the group, grave 180 had other significant attributes. It was the only grave to contain a distinctive fill (181) of burnt red clay with

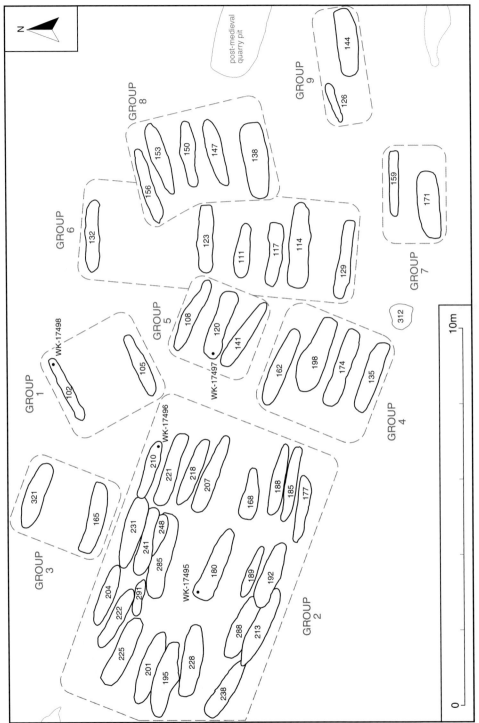

Fig. 5: Plan of the cemetery (scale 1:100)

Fig. 6: The cemetery following excavation, looking west (0.5m scale intervals)

abundant charcoal inclusions, which was clearly evident on the surface before excavation and was found both above and below the skeleton. Grave 180 survived to a depth of 0.3m and contained a moderately well-preserved skeleton, SK182, the remains of an adult female of between 25 and 35 years. The leg bones were found in very unusual positions: the tibia and fibula of the lower right leg were crossed over the femora (upper legs), the bones of the lower left leg were absent, and bones from both feet were lying at the location of the knees (Figs 7 and 8). There was no evidence to suggest that SK182 had been disturbed subsequently, so this peculiar arrangement appears to have been the primary burial disposition. Analysis of the bones revealed that both femora were bowed, the tibia was twisted slightly at the ankle, and the cortices (remains of muscle attachments) were much thicker than usual on the otherwise gracile hand bones. Fill 181 was sampled (as Samples 26 and 32) for the recovery of charcoal and other environmental remains as well as human bone. Sample 26 was taken from fill 181 immediately above SK182, and Sample 32 (divided into 'head' and torso' regions) from immediately below it. Both samples yielded charcoal (see *the charcoal*, below) and a few small fragments of animal bone. SK182 produced a radiocarbon date of 555–655 cal. AD (Wk-17495).

To the north of grave 180 were four intercutting graves: 231, 241, 248 and 285 (Fig. 5). Initially these appeared as a straightforward sequence of burials, from the earliest, grave 285, which contained a moderately well-preserved male adult skeleton (SK287), to the latest, grave 231, which contained a poorly preserved adult female skeleton (SK233). The degree of intercutting between the two central graves, 241 and 248, suggested that grave 241 may have been a deliberate reopening of grave 248. On excavation, however, it became apparent that

Table 1: Summary of all graves, skeletons and dating evidence

Arm positions: A: both arms straight; B: arms crossed on pelvis; C: arms crossed on chest; D: arms crossed on waist; E: right arm behind pelvis, left arm in front of pelvis F: left arm behind pelvis, right arm in front of pelvis; G: both arms behind pelvis; H: right arm on pelvis, left arm on waist; I: left arm on pelvis, right arm on waist; J: right arm on the chest, the left on the pelvis; K: right arm on the pelvis, the left arm on the waist.
Pathology: CO: *cribra orbitalia*; DJD: degenerative joint disease; HFI: *hyperostosis frontalis interna*; NFB: new bone formation; OA: osteoarthritis.

GROUP	Skeleton	Grave	Grave depth	Preservation	Complete-ness	Age at death	Sex	Arm position	Radiocarbon/ other dating	Pathology/condition	Notes
1	104	102	0.12m	poor	50-60%	18-25	f	-	410–560 cal. AD	NBF in skull	
	107	105	0.10m	very poor	60-70%	25-35	f	B	-		
2	170	168	0.04m	very poor	10-20%	2½-4	-	-	-		
	179	177	0.10m	poor	30-40%	35-45	u	-	-	cyst? on tibia	
	182	180	0.30m	moderate	60-70%	25-35	f	K	555–655 cal. AD	Bowed femora and tibia. Tibia twisted at ankle. Thickened cortices on hands	distinctive grave fill. Unusual arrangement of leg bones.
	184	185	0.10m	poor	50-60%	18-25	m?	B	-		
	187	188	0.10m	very poor	50-60%	35-45	u	C	-		
	191	189	0.09m	poor	20-30%	8-17?	-	-	-		buried prone
	194	192	0.19m	poor	30-40%	25-35	f	-	-	HFI	
	197	195	0.28m	poor	35-45%	35-45	f	-	-	HFI. DJD	
	203	201	0.13m	poor	20-30%	35-45	f?	B	-	Thickened cortices on hands	
	206	204	0.06m	poor	0-10%	18+	u	-	-		
	209	207	0.12m	moderate	60-70%	45+	m	H	-	NBF in skull. Stafne's defects	
	212	210	0.08m	poor	60-70%	8-11	-	-	460–650 cal. AD	CO	
	215	213	0.23m	poor	30-40%	45+	m?	-	Roman pottery	DJD	
	217	218	0.04m	very poor	20-30%	18+	u	-	-	thick cranial vault	
	220	221	0.12m	poor	40-50%	35-45	f	-	-	CO	
	224	222	0.05m	very poor	15-25%	6-8½	-	-	-		
	227	225	0.07m	very poor	30-40%	45+	u	-	Late Iron Age/ Early Roman pottery	Paget's disease?	
	230	228	0.19m	poor	50-60%	35-45	f	-	-	DJD. OA. Infected knee	lining/packing stones within grave
	233	231	0.25m	poor	40-50%	35-45	f	A	Roman pottery (BB1)	CO	

Group	SK	Context	Depth	Preservation	%	Age	Sex	Code	Dating	Pathology	Notes
	240	238	0.18m	very poor	60-70%	18-25	f	I	-	DJD. OA	same as SK250
	243	241	0.15m	moderate	30-40%	35+?	m?	-	-	broken finger	
	247	241	0.15m	poor	50-60%	45+	m	C	-		
	250	248	0.10m	moderate	15-25%	35+?	m?	-	-		same as SK243
	287	285	0.22m	moderate	70-80%	18-25	m	E	Iron Age pottery		
	290	288	0.12m	very poor	30-40%	9-12	-	-	-		
	293	291	0.06m	very poor	0-10%	<10?	-	-	-		
3	167	165	0.09m	very poor	30-40%	18+	u	C	-	DJD	
	323	321	0.18m	poor	30-40%	45+	f?	-	-		
4	135	135	0.20m	very poor	60-70%	25-35	f?	C	-	HFI. Broken collar bone.	
	162	162	0.28m	poor	60-70%	18-25	f	C	-		possible foetus/neonate accompanying
	176	174	0.49m	poor	60-70%	25-35	m	G	-	CO. NBF in skull (meningitis?)	
	200	198	0.20m	very poor	50-60%	14-16	-	F	-		
5	108	108	0.10m	poor	55-65%	18-25	m	A	-	CO. broken (lower) leg. Sinusitis	
	122	120	0.20m	moderate	65-75%	18-25	f	D	430–620 cal. AD	CO	
	143	141	0.19m	poor	60-70%	25-35	m	E	Roman pottery	minor toe anomaly	
6	111	111	0.05m	very poor	25-35%	18+	m	-	-		
	114	114	0.10m	very poor	50-60%	25-35	m?	E	-		
	117	117	0.17m	poor	40-50%	6½-8½	-	-	-		
	125	123	0.07m	very poor	25-35%	18-25	u	-	Roman pottery		ironworking slag
	131	129	0.07m	very poor	20-30%	35-45	u	B	-		
	134	132	0.10m	very poor	30-40%	18+	u	-	-		
7	161	159	0.22m	very poor	25-35%	18+	f?	-	-	HFI	
	173	171	0.20m	very poor	40-50%	7-9	-	C	-	CO	
8	140	138	0.15m	very poor	30-40%	45+	u	A	-	DJD. OA	
	149	147	0.10m	very poor	20-30%	18+	u	I	-		
	152	150	0.09m	very poor	50-60%	18+	m?	-	-		
	155	153	0.12m	very poor	5-15%	18+?	u	-	-		
	158	156	0.17m	very poor	5-15%	18+?	u	-	-		
9	128	126	0.04m	very poor	0-5%	<5?	-	-	-		
	146	144	0.20m	very poor	30-40%	18+	f?	J	-		

Fig. 7: Group 2 central grave 180 (SK182), looking south (scale 1m)

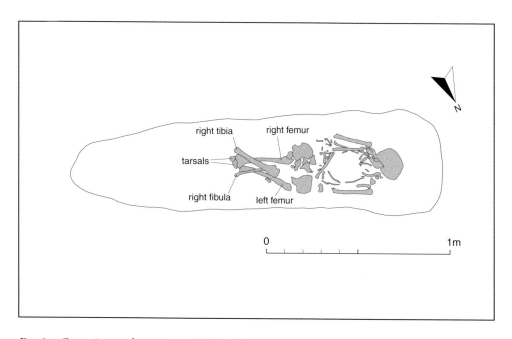

Fig. 8: Group 2 central grave 180 (SK182), plan (scale 1:20)

Fig. 9: Group 2 graves 241 (both SK243 and SK247) and 248 (SK250), looking south (scale 1m)

none of the bones (SK250, including the skull) in grave 248 were *in situ*, and that less than 25% of the skeleton was represented, despite being relatively well preserved. At the same time, additional moderately well-preserved bone (SK243), mostly long bones, was recovered from the excavation of the poorly preserved mature male skeleton (SK247) in grave 241 (Fig. 9). During subsequent analysis it became clear that SK243 and SK250 represented up to 65% of the same moderately well-preserved possible male skeleton. Clearly this burial had been exhumed from grave 248 during the digging of grave 241 and had been partly reburied (as SK243) with SK247. It is not clear if grave 248 was part of an earlier grave into which the rest of the disturbed burial (as SK250) was reinterred, or if it was a niche appended to grave 241 specifically for this purpose. There were also seven foetus or neonate bones associated with SK247 and SK250, probably from another disturbed earlier grave.

To the south of grave 180 were two graves, 189 and 192, which completed the central row of Group 2 burials. The child skeleton (SK191) within grave 189 was the only prone burial in the cemetery. Grave 192 contained a female skeleton; both were poorly preserved.

The eastern row within Group 2 contained eight graves divided into two groups of four. To the north, these contained a male (SK209 within grave 207), a female (SK220 within grave 221), a child (SK212 within grave 210) and an adult skeleton of unknown sex (SK217 within grave 218). Preservation ranged from moderate (SK209) to very poor (SK217), the latter within a grave surviving to a depth of only 0.04m. SK209 showed possible evidence for meningitis and an unusual condition of the jaw known as 'Stafne's Defects' (see *the human bone*, below). Grave 210 appeared to post-date grave 231 at the northern end of the central row. SK212, within grave 210, produced a radiocarbon date of 460–650 cal. AD

Fig. 10:   Group 2 graves 185 (SK184) and 188 (SK187), looking south (scale 1m)

(Wk-17496). Preservation of the skeletons within the four southern graves of this row was either poor or very poor (Fig. 10), and consequently only one possible male (SK184 within grave 185) and a child (SK170 within grave 168) could be identified. Like SK182 within the central grave 180, SK184 also had thick cortices in the hand bones.

All of the ten graves at the western end of Group 2 contained skeletons that were poorly preserved or very poorly preserved. The three central graves (201, 195 and 228) all contained females or possible females aged between 35 and 45. Grave 228 contained a number of undressed stones, most of local limestone but three of yellow sandstone. The stones were concentrated in two areas around the left arm and right leg. To the south were three graves of a possible male of at least 45 years (SK215 within grave 213), a young adult female (SK240 within grave 238) and a child (SK290 within grave 288). All three of these graves appeared to pre-date grave 192 at the southern end of the central row. To the north were four badly truncated graves (204, 222, 225 and 291), none of which survived to more than 0.07m in depth. Sex could not be determined for any of the skeletons within these graves, although two were non-adults, one of which (SK293) lay within the very short grave 291. SK227, within grave 225, was over 45 years of age at death and was found to have thickened skull bones, possibly a case of Paget's disease (see *the human bone*, below).

To the north of Group 2, Group 3 contained two graves, 165 and 321, both orientated north-west/south-east. The graves shared the same alignment as the central row from Group 2, but did not form part of the grouping around the central grave 180. Both skeletons were poorly preserved and could not be confidently sexed, although SK323 within grave 321 was possibly female, over 45 years old.

Fig. 11: Group 4 grave 162 (SK164), looking north-east (scale 1m)

Groups 4 and 5 comprised a row of seven burials approximately 1.5m to the east of Group 2, with which they shared the same approximate orientation. Groups 4 and 5 were separated by a small gap between graves 141 and 162, the latter also being slightly misaligned to the common row. The four graves within Group 4 (135, 162, 174 and 198) were all at least 0.2m deep, and although the skeletons within were poorly preserved they were relatively complete (between 50% and 70%). The skeletons were identified as being one male (SK176), one female (SK164), one possible female (SK137) and a juvenile (SK200). The discovery of four foetus (or neonate) bones with the pelvic and torso bones of SK164, a young adult female, suggests that this could have been the burial of a pregnant woman, or mother with newborn baby (Fig. 11). To the north, Group 5 comprised the moderately well preserved remains of a young adult female (SK122 within grave 120), flanked to either side by poorly preserved male adults. SK122 produced a radiocarbon date of 430–620 cal. AD (Wk-17497).

Group 6 comprised an extended row of six graves, orientated east/west, immediately to the east of Groups 4 and 5 on a north/south alignment. The central four graves were generally more widely spaced than those of Groups 4 and 5, and those to the south (grave 129, 0.7m distant from 114) and north (grave 132, 2.65m distant from 123) were more widely spaced still. Truncation of this group had been considerable, with only one grave (117) surviving to more than 0.1m in depth. Consequently the preservation of the skeletons was generally very poor (Fig. 12): aside from the juvenile (SK119) within grave 117, only one of the other adult skeletons (SK113, a male within grave 111) could be sexed with confidence. Grave 123 yielded a small quantity (20g) of ironworking slag, but not

Fig. 12:   Group 6 grave 123 (SK125), looking south (scale 1m)

enough to indicate the presence of iron smithing or smelting in the near vicinity. Like the pottery, this was probably a residual component of the grave fill.

Group 7 lay to the south-east of Group 6 and comprised two adjacent and parallel east/west-aligned graves. Both were at least 0.2m deep but the skeletons within, those of a child (SK173 within grave 171) aged between 7 and 9 at death, and a possible female (SK161 within grave 159), were very poorly preserved. Grave 171 was unusually wide for the child burial SK173 within.

Group 8 comprised a row of five graves immediately to the east of Group 6. This row was aligned north-north-west/south-south-east, and contained the very poorly preserved remains of five adults, only one of which (SK152 within grave 150) could be tentatively identified as male. The alignment of Group 8 intersected with the alignment of Group 6, although there were no intercutting graves.

To the south-east of Group 8, Group 9 comprised two graves (126 and 144) that lay close together but were not part of a common row. Grave 126 contained the scanty remains of a child (SK128), probably aged under 5 at death; grave 144 contained a possible female. Both skeletons were very poorly preserved.

Undated features (Fig. 4)

Undated features included four pits or postholes, three of which (234, 312, 326) formed an alignment that was coincident with the south-western limit of the cemetery. The fourth possible posthole (236) lay well to the south of this alignment. These features were generally circular, between 0.6m and 1.1m in diameter, and survived to a depth of up to 0.18m. Posthole 312 contained sandstone packing. A total of 14 tree-throw pits were also excavated, one of which (310) produced a single flint flake, presumably of prehistoric date.

THE RADIOCARBON DATES
by Sylvia Warman

Radiocarbon determinations were obtained from the femora of four of the excavated skeletons: SK104 (grave 102); SK122 (grave 120); SK182 (grave 180); and SK212 (grave 210). The primary purpose of the dating programme was to establish the period in which the cemetery was in use, given the paucity of artefactual and other dating evidence. Additionally, it was hoped that the dates obtained might offer an indication of the sequence of cemetery development at least in the western part of the cemetery: poor levels of preservation precluded radiocarbon dating of human bone from the eastern part of the cemetery.

The samples were processed during 2005 at the University of Waikato Radiocarbon Dating Laboratory, Hamilton, New Zealand. For details of methods and equipment used see University of Waikato Radiocarbon Dating Laboratory (2006). The results are conventional radiocarbon ages (Stuiver and Polach 1977) and are given in Table 2, with probabilities presented in Fig. 13. All have been calculated using the calibration curve of Reimer *et al.* (2004) and the computer program OxCal 3.10 (Bronk Ramsey 2005). Date ranges are derived from the probability method (Stuiver and Reimer 1993).

All four samples contained sufficient collagen and were successfully dated. The carbon and nitrogen isotopic ratios are all within the normal range for a largely terrestrial diet (A. Hogg, pers. comm.).

Table 2: Calibrated radiocarbon results

Laboratory No.	Type	Grave	Group	Skeleton	Material	Radiocarbon Age (BP)	Calibrated date range (at 2σ 95.4% confidence)
Wk-17495	AMS	180	2	182	Human femur	1451 +/- 32	555–655 cal. AD
Wk-17496	AMS	210	2	212	Human femur	1491 +/- 30	460 (2%) 490 cal. AD 530 (93.4%) 650 cal. AD
Wk-17497	AMS	120	5	122	Human femur	1515 +/- 32	430–620 cal. AD
Wk-17498	AMS	102	1	104	Human femur	1571 +/- 31	410–560 cal. AD

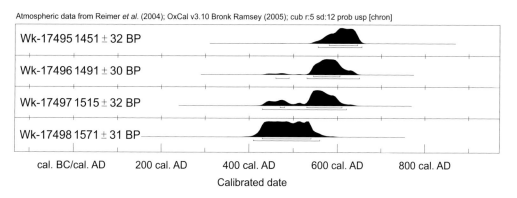

Atmospheric data from Reimer *et al.* (2004); OxCal v3.10 Bronk Ramsey (2005); cub r:5 sd:12 prob usp [chron]

Wk-17495 1451 ± 32 BP

Wk-17496 1491 ± 30 BP

Wk-17497 1515 ± 32 BP

Wk-17498 1571 ± 31 BP

cal. BC/cal. AD   200 cal. AD   400 cal. AD   600 cal. AD   800 cal. AD

Calibrated date

Fig. 13: Probabilities for the radiocarbon determinations

THE HUMAN BONE
by Anwen Caffell and Malin Holst

Introduction

A total of 52 skeletons was recorded during excavation, with one grave (241) thought to contain a double burial (SK243 and SK247). However, grave 241, containing SK247, had been dug through grave 248, containing SK250, and the disturbed bones of SK250 were reburied over the legs of SK247. These disarticulated remains of SK250 were recorded as SK243 during excavation, but it is now clear that SK243 and SK250 are the remains of the same individual and are referred to as such within this report, making a total of 51 skeletons. Very little intercutting was noted between the other graves. In addition, 16 fragments of disarticulated bone not associated with the burials were collected during fieldwork; these have not been subject to analysis.

Methodology

The skeletons were washed carefully and allowed to dry slowly at room temperature over several days. They were then analysed in detail, assessing the preservation and completeness, and determining the age, sex and stature of the individuals. All pathological lesions were also recorded. Comparisons were made with the human remains from other excavated and broadly contemporary cemetery sites from the region, including Henley Wood, North Somerset (67 skeletons, Bayley 1996); Butler's Field, Lechlade, Gloucestershire (222 skeletons, Harman 1998); Beckford cemeteries A and B, Worcestershire (24 and 108 skeletons, Wells 1996); Watchfield, Oxfordshire (43 skeletons, Harman 1992 and Marlow 1992); and with the preliminary analysis from the undated cemetery at Portbury, North Somerset (15 skeletons, Holst 2005).

The human bone report presented here is a summary of the osteological analysis carried out for this group of skeletons. Data relating to the robusticity (*meric*) indices, non-metric traits and full data on dental disease do not appear in this summary. The full report is available in the archive or on demand from Cotswold Archaeology.

Osteological analysis

Preservation and completeness

Preservation (Table 3) was assessed using the seven-category grading system defined by McKinley (2004), ranging from 0 (excellent) to 5+ (extremely poor). Preservation is generally poor (grade 4) to very poor (grade 5), with just over three-quarters (39/51, 76.5%) of the skeletons falling into these two categories. Only five (9.8%) skeletons are in the best preservation grade for this site (moderate, grade 3), where the general surface morphology is retained but detail is masked by erosion over most of the bone surface. Seven (13.7%) skeletons are in the worst preservation category (extremely poor, grade 5+). A large part of the damage suffered by these skeletons was due to extensive root penetration, with many roots removed during washing.

Completeness (Table 4) was assessed using a five-category grading system, ranging from excellent (80–100%) to very poor (0–20%). No skeletons are 80–100% complete, although just under a quarter (12/51, 23.5%) are 60–80% complete. The majority (19/51, 37.3%) are found in the 20–40% complete category, with 11.8% (6/51) in the 0–20% category. As

Table 3: Surface preservation: number and percentage of skeletons in each preservation category according to age and sex

	Excellent		Very Good		Good		Moderate		Poor		Very Poor		Extremely Poor		Total
	0		1		2		3		4		5		5+		
Female	0	0.0%	0	0.0%	0	0.0%	2	12.5%	9	56.3%	4	25.0%	1	6.3%	16
Male	0	0.0%	0	0.0%	0	0.0%	3	25.0%	6	50.0%	3	25.0%	0	0.0%	12
Unsexed	0	0.0%	0	0.0%	0	0.0%	0	0.0%	2	15.4%	8	61.5%	3	23.1%	13
Total Adults	0	0.0%	0	0.0%	0	0.0%	5	12.2%	17	41.5%	15	36.6%	4	9.8%	41
Non-Adults	0	0.0%	0	0.0%	0	0.0%	0	0.0%	3	30.0%	4	40.0%	3	30.0%	10
Total	**0**	**0.0%**	**0**	**0.0%**	**0**	**0.0%**	**5**	**9.8%**	**20**	**39.2%**	**19**	**37.3%**	**7**	**13.7%**	**51**

Table 4: Completeness: number and percentage of skeletons in each completeness category according to age and sex

	Excellent		Good		Moderate		Poor		Very Poor		Total
	80-100%		60-80%		40-60%		20-40%		0-20%		
Female	0	0.0%	6	37.5%	5	31.3%	5	31.3%	0	0.0%	16
Male	0	0.0%	5	41.7%	5	41.7%	2	16.7%	0	0.0%	12
Unsexed	0	0.0%	0	0.0%	1	7.7%	9	69.2%	3	23.1%	13
Total Adults	0	0.0%	11	26.8%	11	26.8%	16	39.0%	3	7.3%	41
Non-Adults	0	0.0%	1	10.0%	3	30.0%	3	30.0%	3	30.0%	10
Total	**0**	**0.0%**	**12**	**23.5%**	**14**	**27.5%**	**19**	**37.3%**	**6**	**11.8%**	**51**

the graves were fully excavated and were not generally truncated by other graves, the low level of completeness of these skeletons reflects the poor preservation at the site.

The poor preservation and incompleteness of many of the skeletons have affected the amount of data it has been possible to retrieve during analysis. This is demonstrated, for example, by the overall high percentage of unsexed adults.

Assessment of Age

Age-at-death was determined using standard ageing techniques after Scheuer and Black (2000a; 2000b) and Cox (2000), which use specific skeletal elements, such as parts of the pelvis, and different stages of bone development and degeneration. Due to poor preservation many of the relevant skeletal elements for assessing age-at-death do not survive. For the majority of the adult skeletons the only means of assessing age-at-death was through dental wear using the methods of Brothwell (1981) and Miles (1962). These age estimations should be viewed with caution as the dental wear is also affected by diet, although as Miles (1962) developed his ageing method based on an Anglo-Saxon population it is likely that the rate of wear exhibited by the Filton skeletons is broadly comparable. For non-adult skeletons the only method of determining age-at-death was through observing dental development (Moorrees *et al.* 1963a; Moorrees *et al.* 1963b), and occasionally dental eruption, where enough of the mandible and maxilla had survived. However, dental development is recognised as an accurate indicator of chronological age as it is less affected by poor nutrition or disease than other indicators, including the development and growth of the skeleton.

Age is split into a number of categories: foetus (up to 40 weeks *in utero*); neonate (around the time of birth); infant (newborn to one year); juvenile (1–12 years); adolescent (13–17 years); young adult (ya; 18–25 years); young middle adult (yma; 26–35 years); old middle adult (oma; 36–45 years); and mature adult (ma; 46+). Adult is used as a category where an individual's age cannot be determined more accurately than that they were 18+. The Filton skeletons comprised 41 adults (80.4%), and 10 non-adults (19.6%). In comparison with other sites the proportion of non-adults is low (although the definition of 'adult' has varied between sites). The closest ratio is from Henley Wood with 15/67 (22.4%) classified as non-adult and 52/67 (77.6%) classified as adults. A recent study (Caffell 2004) has indicated that from Early Saxon cemeteries usually around a third (32.0%) of skeletons are non-adults and around two-thirds (66.6%) are adults, the remainder being un-aged. A considerable proportion of the adult skeletons (12/41, 29.3%) could not be assigned to a more specific age category due to the poor preservation (Table 5). Those adults which could be aged more accurately were reasonably evenly distributed between the four age categories.

Table 5: Number and percentage of adult skeletons in each age category according to sex

%ᵃ: as a percentage of the total individuals in the age category
%ᵇ: as a percentage of the total individuals in the sex category

	YA (18-25)			YMA (26-35)			OMA (36-45)			MA (46+)			A (18+)			Total	
	n	*%ᵃ*	*%ᵇ*	*n*	*%ᵃ*	*%ᵇ*	*n*	*%ᵃ*	*%ᵇ*	*n*	*%ᵃ*	*%ᵇ*	*n*	*%ᵃ*	*%ᵇ*	*n*	*%*
Female	4	50.0%	25.0%	4	57.1%	25.0%	5	62.5%	31.3%	1	16.7%	6.3%	2	16.7%	12.5%	16	39.0%
Male	3	37.5%	25.0%	3	42.9%	25.0%	0	0.0%	0.0%	3	50.0%	25.0%	3	25.0%	25.0%	12	29.3%
Unsexed	1	12.5%	1.0%	0	0.0%	0.0%	3	37.5%	2.9%	2	33.3%	2.6%	7	58.3%	4.5%	13	31.7%
Total	**8**	-	**19.5%**	**7**	-	**17.1%**	**8**	-	**19.5%**	**6**	-	**14.6%**	**12**	-	**29.3%**	**41**	-

Of the non-adult skeletons, three (30%) could not be assigned to a more specific age category, although one (SK128) was probably below the age of 5, another (SK293) was probably below the age of 10, and the other (SK191) was probably between 8 and 17. One of the non-adult skeletons (SK200) was an adolescent aged between 14 and 16 years, and the remaining six were juveniles, one of the latter (SK170) aged between 2½ and 4 years old. A large proportion (6/7, 85.7%) of the Filton non-adults were juveniles, like most of the comparable sites except for Portbury and Henley Wood. However, at Portbury only three non-adult skeletons were identified and different age divisions were used at Henley Wood, where it is likely that some of the individuals classed as 'adolescent' would have been 'juvenile' had the same categories been used. At Watchfield, non-adults were distributed fairly evenly between 'infant', 'juvenile' and 'adolescent' categories. The lack of 'infant' burials at Filton is unusual as all other sites (except Portbury) include at least one, and both foetuses and neonates were recovered from Watchfield and Butler's Field. Although no foetus or neonate burials were identified at Filton, 11 bones from either foetuses or neonates were found as additional material in other graves, including four with the pelvic and torso bones of SK164, a female of 18–25 years, possibly representing a pregnant woman. Several foetal/neonate bones were found with SK243/SK250 and SK247, so it is possible that an earlier neonate grave was disturbed in this area.

Sex determination

Sex was determined using standard techniques following Cox and Mays (2000). Assessment of sex is based primarily on the skull and the pelvis, and can only be carried out once sexual characteristics have developed in older adolescents and adults. The Filton skeletons generally have heavily damaged pelvic bones missing the pubic area, which is the most useful for sex determination. The skulls are generally slightly better preserved, however one skeleton with a very 'female' pelvis has several ambiguous or masculine features on her cranium and mandible, and some other skeletons with 'male' pelves do not display markedly masculine characteristics of the skull. Because of this lack of distinct and consistent sexual dimorphism in the skull, assigning sex to skeletons where only skull bones survive has been generally avoided unless the feminine or masculine traits are very clear.

Sex could not be determined for 13 (31.7%) of the adults, again reflecting the poor preservation. Of the 28 adults which could be sexed, 16 (57.1%) were female (10 female, 6 possibly female), and 12 (42.9%) were male (7 male, 5 possibly male). It is entirely possible that a greater proportion of the unsexed adults were male, which would redress the apparent slight imbalance. Comparable sites show some variation in the ratio of males to females, with the Filton ratio being most similar to Beckford cemetery B and Butler's Field.

Male skeletons that could be aged were evenly distributed between the young, young middle, and mature adult age groups, but there were none in the old middle adult group (Table 5). The female skeletons that could be aged were fairly evenly distributed between the three younger age groups, but there was only one female in the mature adult age group. Although there were broadly similar proportions of males and females in the two younger age groups, a greater proportion of male skeletons were mature adults (33.3%) compared to the small proportion of females (7.1%).

Stature

Stature can usually only be established if at least one complete and fully fused long bone is present. At Filton, none of the long bones were complete, so to gain some idea of stature, long bones have been measured if they have a single clean break with edges fitting tightly together and their ends intact. Although this approach introduces a degree of error it was possible to calculate stature for three females and two males (Table 6).

The female mean height of 1.58m is on the short side for the post-Roman period, which has been calculated at 1.61m (Caffell 1997), and is closer to the mean heights calculated for

Table 6: Stature of females and males, where measurable

Skeleton no.	Stature (cm)	Bone used
Female		
122	163.14 +/- 4.45	humerus
182	150.85 +/- 3.55	femur and tibia
164	160.19 +/- 3.72	femur
mean:	158.06	
Male		
287	176.90 +/- 3.37	tibia
209	175.80 +/- 4.32	radius
mean:	176.35	

the Romano-British (1.57m) or medieval (1.59m) periods (ibid.). The female mean height is shorter than at all the comparable sites, being closest to that for Henley Wood (1.60m). The smallest of the Filton females, at 1.51m, skims the lower end of the range for post-Roman females, but fits comfortably within the range for Romano-British females (ibid.).

In contrast, the male mean height of 1.76m is tall for the post-Roman period, calculated at 1.72m (Caffell 1997). The male mean height is taller than all the comparative sites, the nearest mean heights being from Beckford cemetery A and Watchfield (both 1.73m). Male heights from Anglo-Saxon cemeteries often exceed 180cm, and in Romano-British cemeteries it usually reaches at least 175cm (ibid.), so the two Filton males are comfortably within the Anglo-Saxon range or at the top of the Romano-British range. Of course, the sample size at Filton is very small and so any conclusions drawn must be tentative.

Osteological conclusions

Osteological analysis has confirmed that bones were poorly preserved and no skeletons were complete, but that the cemetery included individuals of both sexes and of all ages. Fewer child and infant skeletons were found than at comparative sites, but this might be due to the poor preservation of the assemblage, as disarticulated neonatal and foetal bones were also recovered. It is possible that infant burials had been particularly shallow, and thus more prone to post-depositional disturbance. The majority of children represented were juveniles, but included one adolescent. The adults were evenly distributed throughout all age categories and tendencies observed at some other sites, such as higher female mortality during childbearing years were not observed. Because of the poor preservation of the skeletal remains it was only possible to calculate stature in a few cases. While the males were taller than the early medieval average, the females were short for the period.

Palaeopathological analysis

Pathological conditions can manifest themselves on the skeleton, especially when these are chronic conditions or the result of trauma to the bone. The bone elements to which muscles attach can also provide information on muscle trauma and excessive use of muscles. The observation of pathological lesions on the skeletons was severely hampered by the poor condition of the bone and incompleteness of the skeletons, to the point where crude prevalence rates would be misleading. Actual prevalence rates, where the number of bone parts affected with a particular condition is divided by the number of the bone parts it was possible to observe, provide a better indication of the occurrence of a pathological lesion, but the fragmentary nature of the remains made this difficult to calculate as lesions may have been unobservable. Both crude and actual prevalence rates are given where possible, to provide a tentative indication of the frequency of diseases present in this population.

Metabolic Conditions

Cribra orbitalia (or fine pitting of the orbital roof) tends to develop during childhood, and often recedes during adolescence or early adulthood. It is thought to be related to iron deficiency anaemia, one of the most common metabolic conditions of the past. The causes of iron deficiency anaemia are complex, and factors affecting its development include environment, hygiene and diet (Stuart-Macadam 1992). *Cribra orbitalia* is often used as an indicator of general stress (Lewis 2000; Roberts and Manchester 1995), and is often found associated with agricultural economies (Roberts and Cox 2003).

Of the 29 individuals with at least one surviving (or partially surviving) orbital roof, 7 (24.1%) showed evidence of *cribra orbitalia*, and 9 of 50 (18.0%) orbital roofs were affected. The condition was much more commonly observed in non-adults, with 3 of 5 (60.0%) having *cribra orbitalia* compared to 16.7% (4/24) of the adults.

Roberts and Cox (2003) report that 7.6% of the early medieval population in Britain (adults and children combined) had *cribra orbitalia*, with 24.6% of orbits affected. Although the proportion of individuals affected at Filton was much higher, the frequency of *cribra orbitalia* in the orbits is actually lower than this, at 18.0%. Little information was available on *cribra orbitalia* in the comparative sites.

Endocrine conditions

Hyperostosis frontalis interna (HFI) appears as irregular nodules of new bone on the internal surface of the frontal bone of the skull, and is believed to be the result of changes in the hormones secreted by the pituitary gland. HFI is almost always seen in females over the age of 30, and has been associated with pregnancy and *acromegaly* (a serious condition that causes the continuation of bone growth in adults whose bones are already fully developed) (Aufderheide and Rodríguez-Martín 1998; Roberts and Manchester 1995).

Four individuals from Filton had small irregular, rounded nodules of new bone on the internal surface of the frontal bone. In all cases these lesions have been interpreted as HFI. All were adult females, two in the young middle adult (25–35 years) age group (SK137 and SK194), one in the old middle adult (35–45 years) group (SK197), and one un-aged (SK161). These age ranges were broadly consistent with the known pattern of HFI manifestation, as it is possible that the two young middle adults were at the upper end of their age group. At least some part of the frontal bone was present in all 16 females, giving a prevalence of 25.0%. HFI is rarely reported in skeletal reports, and was not reported for any of the comparative sites.

Degenerative joint disease

The term 'joint disease' encompasses a large number of conditions with different causes, which all affect the articular joints of the skeleton. Factors influencing joint disease include physical activity, occupation, workload and advancing age, which manifest as degenerative joint disease and osteoarthritis. Joint changes may also have inflammatory causes, such as septic or rheumatoid arthritis.

The most common type of joint disease observed tends to be degenerative joint disease (DJD). DJD is characterised by both bone formation (osteophytes) and bone resorption (porosity) at and around the articular surfaces of the joints, which can cause great discomfort and disability (Rogers 2000). Osteoarthritis is a degenerative joint disease characterised by the deterioration of the joint cartilage, leading to exposure of the underlying bony joint surface. The resulting bone-to-bone contact can produce 'polishing' of the bone. Osteoarthritis can be the result of mechanical stress and other factors, including lifestyle, food acquisition and preparation, social status, sex and general health (Larsen 1997). People with osteoarthritis may (but not always) experience pain and limited movement of the affected joint (Roberts and Manchester 1995).

Nineteen adults (9 females, 7 males, 3 unsexed adults) had at least one fragment of vertebral body surviving, and six (31.6%) of these individuals (3F, 1M, 2U) had at least one body with osteophytes around the margin, coupled with porosity of the body surface. However, the vertebrae were extremely underrepresented, having suffered from poor preservation, and very few fragments of vertebral bodies were actually present. The 45 vertebral bodies recovered equates to an average of 2.5 per skeleton (compared to the original 24 vertebra per body). Ten (22.2%) had evidence of DJD; the prevalence of vertebral bodies affected between males and females was similar. The apophyseal facets, the cartilaginous joints between the vertebrae, also showed evidence of pathology. Of the 1068 facets present, 45 (4.2%) had evidence of DJD, and 1 (0.1%) of osteoarthritis, making a total of 46 (4.3%) facets affected by some type of joint disease. All types of vertebrae were affected. Further evidence for DJD was apparent on 11 of the 19 surviving anterior atlas facets for the odontoid process of the axis, and on 5 of the 18 odontoid processes present. Two individuals had some evidence of DJD in the limb joints: SK197 (right hip, and possibly the right knee and both hands) and SK167 (hand). Three skeletons had evidence of osteoarthritis in the joints of their limb bones: SK140 (both shoulders and the left hip), SK230 (right knee) and SK247 (right shoulder).

Osteoarthritis and DJD are commonly found in early medieval populations (Roberts and Cox 2003). Osteoarthritis was reported in nine individuals from Watchfield, most often in the spine; three individuals from Beckford A (mainly spine, toes and fingers affected); the vertebrae of two individuals at Beckford B; and at Butler's Field (including three individuals with affected shoulders, five with affected hips, and two with affected knees).

Trauma

Evidence of trauma was limited to three individuals, possibly because of the incomplete and fragmentary nature of the remains: SK137 (broken clavicle), SK250 (broken finger) and SK110 (fibula). The fibula and clavicle are the most commonly fractured bones recorded for early medieval populations, with 7% of both clavicles and fibulae affected (Roberts and Cox 2003). Fractures were rare in the Beckford A (one clavicle, one foot, two toes and one finger) and Beckford B (one clavicle and one ulna) populations. Four individuals at Butler's Field had clavicle fractures, three had fractures of the fibula and two had sustained fractures of hand bones; other fractures reported included those of arm and leg bones as well as ribs. Clavicle fractures were recorded in three individuals from Watchfield, and fractured ribs and arm bones also occurred. Only two individuals at Henley Wood had fractures, both of their left clavicles. The pattern of fractures at Filton seems consistent with those at the other sites, although the prevalence rates for the bones are not known.

Infectious disease

Infectious diseases were common in the past, but for evidence to appear in the skeleton the disease must have been chronic, i.e. persisted for some time before death or recovery. Since most infections are acute, i.e. resolved relatively quickly, most infectious diseases will not result in bone changes (Roberts and Manchester 1995).

Three individuals had evidence for new bone formation on the inner surface of the skull. SK104 had several small areas of grey, slightly porous woven bone, SK200 had two large areas of extensive woven bone formation, possibly the result of meningitis, and SK209 had a small, sharply defined, square plaque of rough lamellar bone. Endocranial lesions are believed to be the result of haemorrhage, or inflammation of the meninges surrounding the brain, and possible causes include infection of the meninges, trauma, tumours, tuberculosis, syphilis and vitamin deficiencies (Lewis 2004). They are more commonly seen in non-adults, possibly because bone changes in response to infection occur more rapidly in children. Endocranial new bone formation does occur infrequently in early medieval populations, and Roberts and Cox (2003) report a prevalence of 0.07%.

Evidence for other infectious disease was rare. SK110 showed evidence of sinusitis in the left maxillary sinus. Roberts and Cox (2003) report that 1.3% of the early medieval British population showed signs of maxillary sinusitis. SK230 had new woven bone on the right femur at the back of the knee, the only example of non-specific infection of the post-cranial skeleton.

Miscellaneous pathology

SK209 had two unusual lesions in the mandible (Fig. 14). A small oval depression was observed on the inner surface of both the left and right parts. These lesions are believed

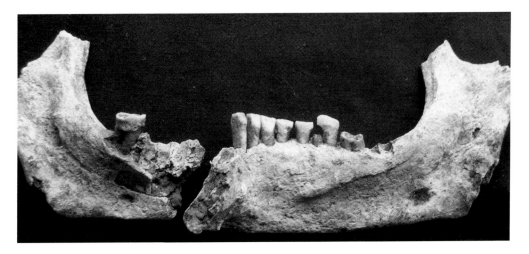

Fig. 14: Mandible of SK209: Stafne's defects

to be Stafne's defects, as described by Lukacs and Rodríguez-Martín (2002). These defects occur more often in males, and are usually seen in middle-aged or older individuals, so this individual fits the normal age and sex profile. Bilateral defects, as occurred here, are much less common than unilateral defects, only occurring in around 13% of individuals with Stafne's defects (ibid.). The prevalence of Stafne's defects among the Filton males was 10% (1/10 mandibles), with 3.3% (1/30 mandibles) of all adults affected. The main cause of Stafne's defects is believed to be an enlarged salivary gland, which either places pressure on the bone surface or secretes substances that cause a limited area of bone to be resorbed.

SK227 (unsexed mature adult) had thickened parietal and occipital skull bones with extremely thin inner and outer skull tables, and the cross section was almost entirely taken up with spongy bone. This is possibly a case of Paget's disease (Aufderheide and Rodríguez-Martín 1998), but without the rest of the skeleton a firm diagnosis is impossible. Paget's disease occurs in elderly people and causes enlargement and distortion of the bones. This can lead to headaches, bone bowing and paralysis (Youngson 1992).

SK182, the adult female within central grave 180, had bowing of the leg bones. Both femora were bowed, the muscle attachments along the backs of the femora were pronounced and the cortices were thick and solid, although the bone externally appeared relatively small and gracile (Fig. 15). Unusually thick cortices were also observed in the hand bones (metacarpals and phalanges). The right tibia was also curved, and the ankle end was twisted sideways. The right fibula appeared to be straight, as were the bones of the upper limbs. The left lower leg was absent.

Thick cortical bone appeared to be a feature of the Filton population, and affected a large number of different bone elements. Several skeletons, including SK182 and SK184,

Fig. 15: Bowed right femur of SK182

had unusually thick cortices in the metacarpals and hand phalanges (finger bones), yet outwardly the bones had a delicate and gracile appearance. This tendency for thick cortices probably indicates a physically active lifestyle. Other pathology included a possible cyst on the right tibia of SK179, and a small defect in the big toe of SK143.

Palaeopathological conclusions

Despite the poor preservation of the skeletal remains, evidence of disease and trauma could be observed. The most common pathological conditions included degenerative changes observed in the vertebrae and other joints. Osteoarthritis was observed in three individuals, in the shoulders, hips and knees. Trauma was largely concentrated on the upper limb and included a clavicle fracture, a finger fracture and muscular trauma. The joint disease and trauma are both likely to be activity-related.

Evidence for physical stress during childhood was observed in the form of pitted eye orbits and grooves on the teeth. Factors causing these conditions may have contributed to the deaths of the nine juveniles buried at Filton. It is possible that the adolescent died of meningitis, or another disease related to inflammation of the meninges surrounding the brain. This condition was also observed in one of the adults. One male had suffered from chronic sinusitis, which might have been caused by smoky living conditions. Another individual may have suffered from Paget's disease, which is characterised by thickening and distortion of the bones and can lead to symptoms from headaches to paralysis. Stafne's defects were a particularly unusual condition observed. These are indentations on the inside of the lower jaw, which might be related to salivary gland anomalies or might be stress indicators.

Dental disease

Analysis of teeth from archaeological populations provides clues about health, diet and oral hygiene, as well as information about environmental and congenital conditions. Thirty-seven adults and eight non-adults had surviving teeth. Of the 839 tooth positions present in the adult skeletons, 707 permanent teeth were preserved, plus one retained deciduous molar. Sixty-seven teeth were lost post-mortem, 49 were lost ante-mortem and 15 were either unerupted or not present. Amongst the non-adult skeletons, 46 deciduous tooth positions contained 45 deciduous teeth (one tooth lost post-mortem), and 76 permanent tooth positions contained 67 erupted permanent teeth (nine lost post-mortem); an additional 74 unerupted permanent teeth were present.

Calculus

All 37 adults, and six non-adults, had accumulations of mineralised dental plaque (calculus), a condition commonly observed in archaeological populations whose dental hygiene was not as rigorous as it is today. As is usual, the prevalence of calculus increased with age and heavy calculus accumulations were found in individuals in the two older age groups. Females tended to be more affected by calculus than males. This is contrary to modern populations, where men tend to have more and heavier calculus deposits than women (Hillson 1996). The adolescent, SK200, had moderate to heavy concretions on several teeth, which is unusual for such a young individual. This could indicate that this child had practised poor oral hygiene, or could possibly indicate a period of sickness before death. Notably, this individual had extensive endocranial new bone formation, probably a result of inflammation of the layers of connective tissue surrounding the brain (above).

Dental caries

Dental caries (tooth decay) was observed in 42 (5.9%) of the 707 adult permanent teeth, and 17 (45.9%) adults were affected. None of the non-adults had carious lesions. The percentage of both individuals and teeth with caries increased with age, with 12.4% (15/121) of the teeth from mature adults having cavities compared to only 2.0% (4/198) of the teeth from young adults. Females usually have a higher caries prevalence rate than males, but at Filton the male teeth had a slightly higher prevalence rate (5.6% or 14/248) than female teeth (4.1% or 14/339). Most of the lesions were small or medium-sized holes where the crown meets the root, which is typical of the early medieval period. Moore and Corbett (1971) suggest that this pattern of caries location results from the collection of food debris around the gum-line, and that this may be related to heavy tooth wear. The levels of calculus (above) certainly suggest that no real effort was made to remove food debris from the mouth.

A recent study of dental caries in early medieval Britain found that the prevalence rate in adult permanent teeth in the Early Saxon period (5th to mid 7th centuries) was 3.9%, with 3.8% of male teeth and 4.3% of female teeth having carious lesions (Caffell 2004). The overall prevalence rate at Filton was slightly higher than this, but was still low in comparison with later periods (ibid.). The caries prevalence at other sites in the south-west of Britain was variable. At Beckford A and B caries prevalence in teeth was extremely low, at 0.4% and 0.14% respectively, whereas prevalence rates at Watchfield and Henley Wood were much higher, at 8.7% and 10.3% respectively. The rate at Butler's Field (6.2%) was closest to that seen at Filton.

Abscesses

Dental abscesses were observed in 10 adult individuals (27.0%), and 13 (1.5%) of the surviving 839 tooth positions. Individuals in the mature adult age group were more likely to be affected by a dental abscess, with 66.7% (4/6) of individuals and 5.1% (7/138) of the tooth positions affected. These frequencies were markedly higher than those in other age groups. Male individuals (5/10, 50%) and male tooth positions (6/270, 2.2%) were more commonly affected by abscesses than were female individuals (2/16, 12.5%) and tooth positions (2/421, 0.5%). All abscesses occurred in the mandible, although in most cases the maxilla had not survived or was extremely fragmented.

The prevalence of abscesses at Filton was similar to that observed in a study of several early medieval sites, which found 2.8% tooth positions were affected (Roberts and Cox 2003). As with caries prevalence, a very low abscess prevalence of 0.4% was observed at Beckford A; although abscesses were also present at Beckford B, a prevalence rate could not be calculated. Six of eight adults were recorded as having abscesses at Watchfield, but no absolute prevalence for tooth positions was given.

Ante-mortem tooth loss

Ante-mortem tooth loss (AMTL) can occur as a result of a variety of factors, including dental caries, pulp-exposure from heavy tooth wear, or periodontal (gum) disease. Once the tooth has been lost, the empty socket is filled in with bone. AMTL was observed in eight adults (21.6%), and affected 49 (5.8%) of the surviving 839 tooth positions. It was only seen in individuals in the two older age groups, reflecting heavier tooth wear and a higher prevalence of dental caries and abscesses. In two individuals the mandible was practically toothless. The rate of AMTL at Filton was slightly lower than the 8% reported for several sites from the early medieval period (Roberts and Cox 2003). The prevalence of AMTL at Henley Wood and Beckford A was much lower, at 2.2% and 2.8% respectively.

Enamel hypoplasia
Dental enamel hypoplasia (DEH) is the manifestation of lines, grooves or pits on the surface of the tooth crown, which represent a period when crown formation is halted. These defects are caused by periods of severe stress, such as episodes of malnutrition or disease, during the first to seventh year of childhood. DEH was uncommon, being recorded in only 2.1% (15/707) of the permanent teeth from adults, and 16.4% (11/67) permanent teeth from non-adults. Six adults and one non-adult had teeth affected, predominantly as a faint line in the enamel. It is possible that the condition that had caused the DEH lines in the child had also contributed to this individual's death. The visibility of DEH may be affected by calculus obscuring enamel defects. This could partly explain why the prevalence at Filton is so much lower than the 7.4% of teeth affected recorded for several early medieval sites (Roberts and Cox 2003).

Dental Anomalies
Other dental anomalies included unerupted teeth (all third molars), peg teeth, impacted molars, crowding and rotation of teeth, enamel pearls and a retained deciduous tooth.

Dental Conclusions
The dentitions of the Filton skeletons had not suffered as severely from erosion as the bones, which meant that the quantity and quality of dental disease in this population was more clearly evident than that of bone pathology. Tooth decay, abscesses, ante-mortem tooth loss and mineralised plaque were noted in many individuals and increased in frequency with age. While cavities were fairly typical of the period and generally low, heavy wear of the teeth was common, leading to abscesses and ante-mortem tooth loss. Oral hygiene was poor, resulting in plaque concretions, even on children's teeth.

Conclusions

Osteological analysis has established that this was a mixed group of adults and children. The children were mainly juveniles (1 to 12 years), but one adolescent (14 to 16 years) was present. Several foetal/neonate bones were also found associated with other skeletons, indicating that at least two foetuses or newborn babies were buried in the cemetery. The adults were fairly evenly distributed between all the age groups. Although more females than males were identified, the ratio did not differ significantly from that normally expected. Due to poor preservation, it was impossible to determine the age or sex of several adults.

It was only possible to calculate stature for a small number of individuals. The females seem short for the early medieval period, and they also seem to be rather gracile, but the males were taller than the early medieval average height.

Filton is most similar to Henley Wood in terms of the proportions of adults and children, and in terms of the height of the female skeletons. However, it differs from Henley Wood in terms of the age distribution of the children, the proportions of males and females, and male stature. In terms of child age distribution and the ratio of males and females,

Filton is more similar to Beckford and Butler's Field; in terms of male stature, it is closest to Beckford A and Watchfield. However, the poor preservation of the Filton skeletons has severely restricted the reconstruction of stature and samples were exceedingly small.

Evidence for a variety of pathological conditions was observed. Degenerative changes were observed in the vertebrae of several individuals, as well as in other joints. Osteoarthritis was observed in the shoulders of two individuals, one of whom also had osteoarthritic changes of the hip, and in the knee of another. Trauma was observed in three individuals, one with a fractured clavicle (collar bone), another with a fractured hand phalanx (finger) and the third with a fractured fibula (lower leg).

Several individuals had *cribra orbitalia*, and a few had *dental enamel hypoplasia* (enamel defects), both lesions that suggest episodes of childhood stress, such as disease or malnutrition. Evidence for infection was seen in a few individuals, notably a young adult and an adolescent with new bone formation on the internal surface of the cranium, indicative of inflammation of the meninges surrounding the brain. This might have resulted from meningitis, but other causes are possible and should be considered. One male showed evidence of sinusitis, maybe a reflection of smoky living conditions.

Several dental diseases were also observed, including dental caries (tooth decay), abscesses, ante-mortem tooth loss and calculus (mineralised plaque). As might be expected, these conditions all increased in frequency with age. The caries prevalence is reasonably low and typical of the period, when most people would have been eating locally produced food, with cereals (wheat, rye, barley and oats) in the form of bread, pottage and ale forming the mainstay of the diet, supplemented with pulses, a limited range of vegetables, fruits and berries, dairy produce and some meat and fish (Hagen 1992; Hagen 1995). Although the carbohydrate content of the diet was high, these were not refined and most of the bread eaten was coarse, meaning that they were unlikely to cause the development of tooth decay. That tooth decay did occur testifies that some sugars were present in the diet, probably in fruits and vegetables, dried fruits and honey. The fact that the caries prevalence was similar between males and females suggests they ate a similar diet. The dental abscesses and ante-mortem tooth loss observed were probably the result of heavy wear of the teeth and dental caries. In both cases the frequency is in keeping with that generally observed in the early medieval period. Accumulations of calculus on their teeth strongly suggest that oral hygiene was poor, and cleaning teeth was not a priority.

The presence of Stafne's defects in the mandible of a male is notable. These are rarely reported in the anthropological literature, and the bilateral form seen here is particularly uncommon. One skeleton had thickening of the cranial vault that could possibly be ascribed to Paget's disease, which is also rarely reported from archaeological contexts, and another had bowed leg bones, of unknown cause.

THE CHARCOAL
by Rowena Gale

Charcoal fragments were recovered from context 181 (as samples 26 and 32), the distinctive, charcoal-rich fill surrounding SK182 within grave 180. The charcoal fragments are mostly very small and only a few pieces measure 2mm or more in radial cross-section. The wood structure is well preserved and firm. The samples were prepared and examined using standard methods (Gale and Cutler 2000). Where possible, the maturity of the wood has been assessed (i.e. heartwood/sapwood). The results are presented in Table 7.

The charcoal consists of a mixture of species including mostly oak (some from mature wood) but also ash, blackthorn and the hawthorn/*Sorbus* group (Pomoideae). Charred hazel nutshell is also present. Fragments of both slow and fast-grown oak are present. The absence of hazel wood may be attributable to the general paucity of charcoal fragments of suitable size for identification. Had the nuts been attached to branches at the time of burning this would indicate a late summer or autumn burial. However, it is feasible that nutshell was added independently and since whole nuts can be stored indefinitely, the season of the year in which the burning took place cannot be deduced.

Table 7: Charcoal results

Sample no.	No. of fragments	Family/species	common name	comments
32 (skull)	8	*Quercus* sp.	oak	too small to assess maturity
	1	*Fraxinus excelsior*	ash	heartwood
	2	Pomoideae	hawthorn/*Sorbus* group	-
32 (torso)	9	*Quercus* sp.	oak	heartwood and unknown maturity
	2	*Quercus* sp.	oak	sapwood
	2	*Prunus spinosa*	blackthorn	-
	2	*Corylus avellana*	hazel	nutshell
Wk-17497	7	*Quercus* sp.	oak	sapwood
	5	*Quercus* sp.	oak	heartwood and unknown maturity
	1	*Prunus spinosa*	blackthorn	-

DISCUSSION

by Anwen Caffell, Kate Cullen, Malin Holst and Martin Watts

Excavation revealed the poorly preserved remains of a small and relatively compact and apparently isolated cemetery of 51 burials situated on a north-west facing hillside. Although some Roman and Late Iron Age pottery was recovered from a few of the graves, four radiocarbon dates obtained from human bone indicate that the cemetery was in use in the early medieval period and that all recovered pottery was residual. The radiocarbon date from grave 102 shows that burial had commenced by the mid 6th century AD at the latest. The dates obtained from graves 120, 180 and 210 suggest that burial had ceased by the early to mid 7th century, although the eastern part of the cemetery remains undated and burial there could have continued into the 8th century, and possibly beyond. Thus it is conceivable that the cemetery was in use for a comparatively short period of time in the 6th century, or burial could have been ongoing for 200 years or longer from the early 5th century onwards.

Spatial distributions

The interpretative groups of graves within the cemetery are based solely on the spatial patterning of the graves, primarily from the presence of rows of burials and their differing alignments across space, but also from clusters of burials and rows. Other recorded attributes were considered, including sex, age and arm positions, and although there were some hints of trends, none were strong enough to affect the interpretative groupings. Consideration of all of these attributes was greatly hindered by non-identification from the poor survival of many skeletons, particularly towards the north-east of the cemetery.

Males, females and children were found in all parts of the cemetery (Fig. 16). From those whose sex could be identified, there was a slight tendency for females to be found in the western half, with males in the eastern half, however, the high number of unsexed individuals renders this apparent trend insignificant. Likewise, the slight tendency for older adults to be buried in the western part of the cemetery and younger adults in the eastern half (Fig. 17) cannot be taken as significant, given the difficulties in identifying the age of many of the adult skeletons. Highly localised trends appear where these tendencies coincide, for example, both burials in Group 1 are young or young middle adult females, and there is a small group of three old middle adult females at the western end of Group 2 (in graves 195, 201 and 228) but these are not strong enough or widespread enough to be statistically significant. Likewise, the possible presence of paired mother-and-child burials in both Groups 7 and 9 may be inferred, but remains unproven.

No trends were apparent in the distribution of the various arms positions (Fig. 18). This is not surprising given the poor survival at Filton and the conclusions of a wider study of arm positions in a selection of Late Roman and early post-Roman cemeteries, which found no general chronological or spatial patterning of the different specific positions could be perceived (Woodward 1993, 224). It may be significant that the most common arm position was C, with arms crossed on the chest. It has been suggested that this position might be a possible indicator of Christianity, although this is far from certain (Rahtz *et al.* 2000, 417).

Organisation and development of the cemetery

The identification of several groups of burials, based on rows, orientations and relative

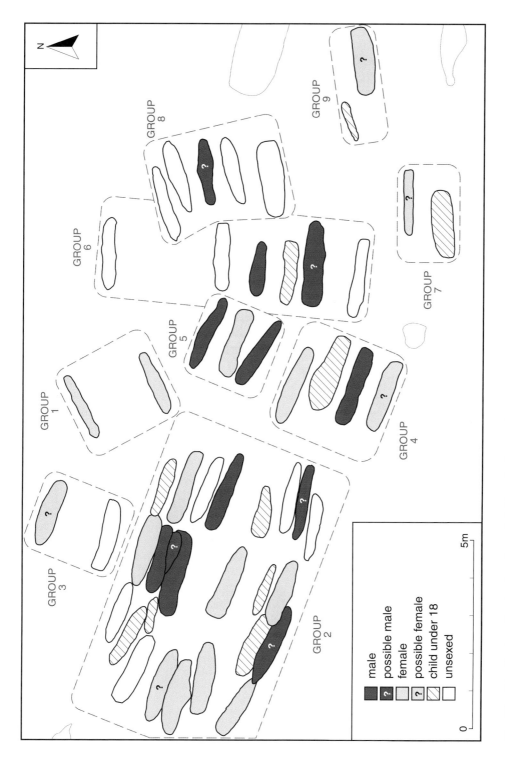

Fig. 16: Distribution of males, females and children (scale 1:100)

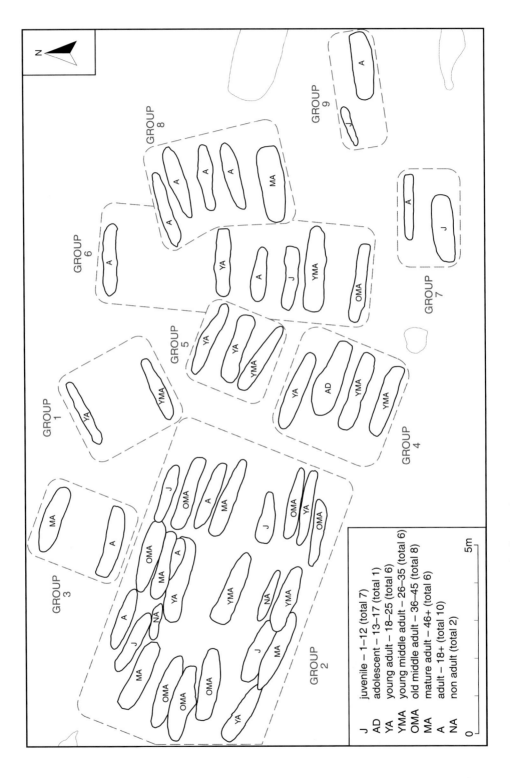

Fig. 17: Distribution of age groups (scale 1:100)

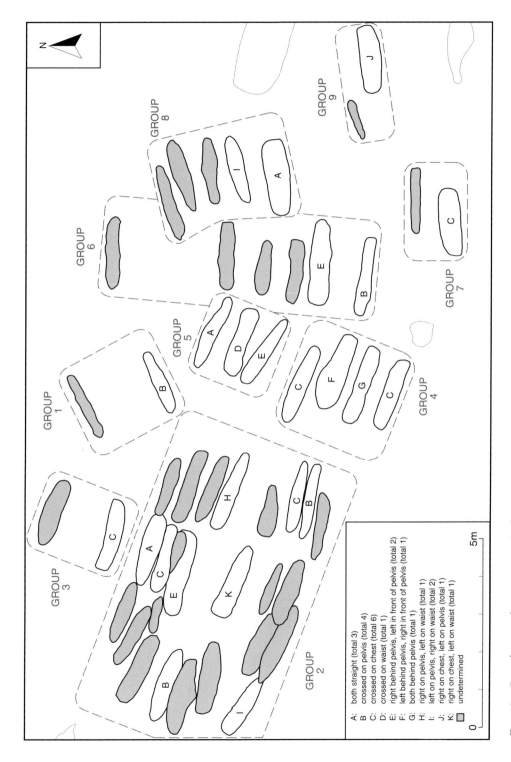

A: both straight (total 3)
B: crossed on pelvis (total 4)
C: crossed on chest (total 6)
D: crossed on waist (total 1)
E: right behind pelvis, left in front of pelvis (total 2)
F: left behind pelvis, right in front of pelvis (total 1)
G: both behind pelvis (total 1)
H: right on pelvis, left on waist (total 1)
I: left on pelvis, right on waist (total 2)
J: right on chest, left on pelvis (total 1)
K: right on chest, left on waist (total 1)
□ undetermined

0   5m

Fig. 18: Distribution of arm positions (scale 1:100)

positions, aids understanding of the layout of the cemetery, but not necessarily of its development. Given the dearth of stratigraphic relationships, dating evidence and grave goods, and the apparent lack of meaningful spatial distributions of skeletal attributes, it is not possible to determine a precise chronology within the cemetery. There is evidence, however, that can provide some insight into how it may have developed.

It seems likely that a common orientation of graves provides an indication of relative contemporaneity within the cemetery. Therefore it may be argued that Groups 2, 3, 4 and 5, with a common grave orientation of north-east/south-west, are probably broadly contemporary (Fig. 5). Conversely, groups on different alignments were probably not in use at the same time, particularly where those alignments appear to cut across each other (Groups 5, 6 and 8). It may also be argued that Groups 7 and 9 are broadly contemporary, given that both contain two closely lying graves of a female and child on similar orientations in the same part of the cemetery. Thus it may be possible to deduce five separate phases of cemetery development: Group 1; Groups 2, 3, 4 and 5; Group 6; Groups 7 and 9; and Group 8. The lack of stratigraphic relationships severely curtails any attempt to identify a relative chronology between these phases, although the radiocarbon dates provide some indication (Table 2; Figs 5 and 13). Although there is some overlap between all of them, Group 1 grave 102 (410–560 cal. AD, Wk-17498), dating from the 5th to mid 6th century, is almost certainly earlier than Group 2 grave 180 (555–655 cal. AD, Wk-17495) dating from the mid 6th to mid 7th century. By extension, Group 1 is also probably earlier than Groups 3, 4 and 5, and may well represent the earliest phase of the cemetery. The similarity of dates obtained from Group 2 grave 180 and Group 2 grave 210 (530–650 cal. AD at 93.4% confidence, Wk-17496) supports the inclusion of these graves in the same group. Although the long date range obtained from Group 5 grave 120 (430–620 cal. AD, Wk-17497) indicates a possible 5th-century date, the probability graph (Fig. 13) shows a 6th-century date as being most likely, supporting the association of Groups 2 and 5 on the basis of a shared orientation. The relative chronology of Groups 6 to 9 cannot be determined; however, assuming there was continuity of use of the cemetery, the lack of a substantial overlap between the Group 1 radiocarbon determination and those obtained for Groups 2 and 5 could indicate that undated Groups 6 to 9 were in use between these dated phases. Such a chronology might also be represented through grave orientation, with the north-east/south-west orientation of Group 1 developing through Groups 8 and 9 to the east/west orientation of Group 6, prior to the predominant north-west/south-east orientation of Groups 2 to 5. Thus it appears that Group 2, with burials clustered around a special central grave, is unlikely to have been the earliest phase of the cemetery, and could have been one of the last.

There are a number of possible reasons for the presence of gaps within some rows of burials. It may be that these gaps represent the locations of shallow graves that did not survive subsequent ploughing at all, although the relative lack of residual bone in the excavated graves and topsoil suggests that was probably not a common occurrence. Perhaps more likely is that these were vacant plots, possibly reserved for specific individuals who were ultimately buried elsewhere. At Tolpuddle Ball, Dorset, similar gaps were recognised in some rows, and it was considered that these gaps might originally have contained the graves of young infants dug to a shallower depth than those of adults (Hearne and Birbeck 1999, 227). A similar explanation is possible here, given the poor representation of infant graves and the presence of infant bones in other graves (see above). It is also possible that, where rows intersect, gaps were left to avoid earlier graves (e.g. the gap between graves 123 and 132 in Group 6 avoiding grave 156 in Group 8).

The gaps between burials within Group 2 appear to be structured and suggest that there were above-ground features to assist with the management of this part of the cemetery. The most obvious is that around grave 180, which sets this central grave apart from all others in the group. This may have been a result of a structure built over or around it, or possibly an earthen mound, which could account for its better survival and lack of disturbance by later graves. Although no other evidence for grave markers was identified, the dearth of intercutting graves would suggest that each grave remained visible throughout the use of the cemetery, possibly from markers made of perishable material. The gap to the north of grave 180 appears to extend in both directions, to the north of graves 201 to the west and 168 to the east. Given the otherwise tight placing and occasional intercutting of adjacent graves this gap might be indicative of a pathway. A possible fence along the southern edge of Groups 2 and 4 is represented by postholes 312, 234 and 326 (Fig. 5), and it is possible that Group 2 was entirely enclosed in this manner.

Despite a complete lack of dating evidence, the distribution of tree-throw pits may indicate the former presence of a small copse that was contemporary with the cemetery, perhaps providing a focus for the siting of the cemetery. Other than the tree-throw pits, the cemetery appears to have been an isolated feature of the early medieval landscape, with no trace of contemporary settlement or other activity in the immediate area. The modern layout of field boundaries clearly has some antiquity, but there is no coincidence with the alignment of the cemetery, and particularly the posthole alignment along its southern side, to suggest any continuity between the early medieval cemetery and the later medieval farmsteads of the vicinity.

Population

Despite the limitations of poor survival it is clear that the cemetery contained a mixed group of adults and children, and with no evidence to suggest selective burial these may be considered as representative of the local population of the 5th to 7th centuries AD.

Where preservation has allowed, the skeletons highlight interesting differences to other cemetery groups of the period and region. In particular the shorter-than-average females and larger-than-average males may indicate this particular trait was displayed purely within this population, or that individuals originated from differing regions or sectors of the community. However, it was only possible to calculate stature for an exceedingly small number of individuals (Table 6), and female stature is heavily skewed by SK182, who was considerably shorter than the other two females. Although a female height of 151cm is not abnormally short for the period, if SK182 is excluded the female mean stature rises to almost 162cm, very similar to the Anglo-Saxon mean.

A variety of pathological conditions was observed, including degenerative joint disease and osteoarthritis, which give some indication as to the diet and overall health of the population. Few instances of trauma were apparent but included a broken collar bone, lower leg and a finger, all common injuries within early medieval populations. The joint disease and trauma were probably related to activity, and other features of the population such as thick cortices also indicate that these people led physically active lives. This would be expected in a population engaged in subsistence farming. The occurrence of *cribra orbitalia* and *dental enamel hypoplasia* suggest childhood disease or malnutrition. As well as small stature, the combination of conditions on SK182 is notable and includes bowed femora and right tibia (the left one was missing), with a slight twisting of the tibia at the ankle. It is unclear why these conditions occurred or how noticeable they would have been in life.

The presence of Stafne's defects in the mandible of a male is notable. These are rarely reported in the anthropological literature, and the bilateral form seen here is particularly uncommon. One skeleton had thickening of the cranial vault that could possibly be ascribed to Paget's disease, which is also rarely reported from archaeological contexts. Several dental diseases were also observed, all of which increased in frequency with age. The caries prevalence is reasonably low and typical of the period.

Mortuary practice

All individuals were buried in extended and supine positions, bar one non-adult (SK191) who was buried extended and prone, and one adult male (SK243/SK250) whose body position could not be ascertained as the skeleton was disarticulated. One grave (228) showed some evidence for a possible stone lining. No coffin nails or evidence for any other grave furniture were retrieved, or any grave goods of any type.

Within the cemetery, the burial of SK182 within grave 180 stands out as being special in numerous ways. Unlike all of the other surviving burials, which after interment appeared to have been filled with the material removed to create the grave, grave 180 contained a highly distinctive fill of burnt clay and charcoal. It was one of the deeper surviving graves and the distinctive fill appeared not to have been disturbed by later activity, therefore the unusual placing of the bones of the lower right leg and feet, and absence of bones from the lower left leg, appear to have been primary and deliberate. There was no pragmatic reason to treat the body in this way as the grave was easily large enough to have accommodated this rather diminutive individual fully extended (Fig. 8). While it is possible that the bowed and twisted condition of this individual's leg bones may have been the impetus for this unusual practice it would be virtually impossible to prove, and there are no known parallels that the authors are aware of, either archaeological or ethnographic. Study of the charcoal recovered from the fill of grave 180 has identified a mixture of species, including mostly oak (some from mature wood) but also ash, blackthorn and the hawthorn/*Sorbus* group. It is clear that this is the grave of a highly distinctive young woman who had particular significance, being at the centre of Group 2 but separate from all the surrounding burials, and having an apparently unique mortuary practice.

The context of the cemetery, by Neil Holbrook

The discovery of a cemetery in south Gloucestershire which radiocarbon dating shows fully to fall into the post-Roman period is significant. Post-Roman cemeteries that are culturally quite distinct from Anglo-Saxon influenced burials are a well-known and distinctive facet of the archaeology of South-West England and Wales. In England they are best known in Somerset at sites such as Cannington (Rahtz *et al.* 2000) and Henley Wood (Watts and Leach 1996), although other important cemeteries have been found in east Devon at Kenn (Weddell 2000); Dorset at Tolpuddle Ball and Ulwell (Hearne and Birbeck 1999; Cox 1988), and throughout Wales (James 1992). Until 2005 such burials had not been positively identified in England north of the Bristol Avon, although there are number of possible candidates in the Bristol region. At Blaise Castle, 5km west of Filton, it is likely that a Roman temple was constructed within the bounds of an Iron Age hillfort (Rahtz and Clevedon Brown 1959). The structure was surrounded by inhumation burials that are no earlier than late Roman, and quite conceivably post-Roman by analogy with Henley Wood where post-Roman burials were dug into the ruins of a Roman temple (Watts and Leach 1996). On Kings Weston Hill, 1km to the south-west of Blaise Castle, a group of eight or more east/west-aligned burials, with heads to the west, were exposed in a pipe trench in 1966. No dating evidence was recovered (Godman 1972). Another possible site lies 5km to the south of Filton in the St George area of east Bristol, where burials have been found in 1894 and 2002, one of which has produced a radiocarbon date of 1573 ± 68 BP (Wk-1396) which calibrated at 95% confidence produces a date of 340–640 cal. AD (Williams 2004; Jones 2006, 192). A fourth possible site was discovered in 1910 on the summit of Tytherington Hill, 12km north-east of Filton, and close to The Castle Iron Age hillfort. Here quarrying revealed 12 extended inhumations arranged in two rows with heads pointing to the west. No artefacts were recovered. Whether further burials were destroyed without record is uncertain (Pritchard 1911, 66–7). In all cases further work will be required before we can ascertain whether the cemeteries were late Roman, post-Roman or indeed span both periods.

The Filton cemetery of 51 individuals was in use for some period of time from the early 5th to the mid 7th century or later. Just how long burial was being carried out is impossible to say on current evidence. Its use might date entirely to the 6th century or significantly longer. We could be dealing with the burial ground of a single extended family or selected individuals from a much larger community. The demographic composition of the cemetery does not favour a selected population, however, and the layout of the graves suggests that the cemetery developed over a period of time. An interpretation of the cemetery as the burial ground of a kin group that was in use for at least a century is therefore to be preferred.

There are suggestions that the south-western boundary of the cemetery was defined by a fence, and the tree-throw holes indicate that the area was at least partly wooded at some date. No such holes were cut by any of the graves so the trees were either contemporary with, or later than, the cemetery. Extensive evaluation demonstrates that no settlement (or at least one that has left any archaeological trace) lay in the immediate vicinity of the cemetery (although it is possible that other small, similar burial plots located between evaluation trenches may have been missed). This apparent absence is typical of the post-Roman period, where settlement sites are hardly known and certainly not in immediate proximity to cemeteries. The settlement pattern in this part of the Severn Vale in the late Roman period was characterised by small farmsteads such as that examined at Stoke Gifford, 2km to the north (Parker 1978; Holbrook 2006). Poorly documented Roman remains and finds are recorded in the general vicinity of the cemetery, near Stoke House and at the Hewlett Packard complex (see *Introduction*, above), but no trace of later activity is recorded at any of these sites. The absence of evidence for earlier remains at the cemetery is noteworthy: a common feature of sub-Roman cemeteries in western Britain is their location adjacent to ruined but visible Romano-British villas and temples, or inserted in and around prehistoric earthworks (cf. James 1992).

A final point regarding the location of the cemetery is that it lies in the south-west corner of the parish of Stoke Gifford, close to the boundaries recorded in the 19th century with the neighbouring parishes of Filton to the west and Stapleton to the south. The current limit of Stoke Gifford parish immediately to the west and south of the cemetery is a recent boundary change (Fig. 1). Desmond Bonney (1966) observed several decades ago that some pagan Saxon burials in Wiltshire lie on the lines later adopted as parish boundaries, while the post-Roman cemeteries at Tolpuddle Ball, Dorset, and Stoneage Barton, Somerset, amongst others, also lie close to parish boundaries (Hearne and Birbeck 1999, 230–1; Webster and Brunning 2004, 77). Filton is another possible example of this phenomenon, although the significance and interpretation of this juxtaposition is still unclear.

The cemetery displays a number of elements that are common to post-Roman cemeteries in western Britain and southern Scotland. It contains a number of paired burials (Groups 1, 3, 7 and 9) which do not conform to the ordered rows otherwise apparent. It is possible these burials were enclosed by hedge banks or fences that have left no trace but served at the time to separate these burials from other interments in the cemetery. The most significant aspect of the cemetery is the 'special' or 'nuclear' grave 180 containing a woman in her late twenties or early thirties, which has a number of unusual aspects. Prior to burial, both legs of the body had been removed below the knee, and the left foot (and possibly the right foot) detached from the ankle. Presumably dismemberment was undertaken with a knife or blade, although no cut marks were apparent on any of the surviving leg or ankle bones. The left lower leg was not placed in the grave (perhaps it was retained by the community as a venerated relic?) while the right leg was placed above the upper legs. Upon discovery the tibia and fibula were found in a cross, which implies that the bones were cut from the flesh before being placed in the grave separately. An alternative (and perhaps more plausible) explanation is that the severed leg was placed in the grave shortly after dismemberment, and that the bones moved out of their original articulation during post-burial settlement (no evidence of animal disturbance was found). Other evidence for post-burial settlement within the grave included the right femur, which had turned (or rolled) inwards. Both feet were placed in the grave by the knees, the right foot possibly still attached to the lower right leg. The grave cut was filled with burnt red clay containing abundant charcoal quite distinct from the clean fills of the other graves, possibly the sweepings from a bonfire lit as part of the funeral ritual.

Few parallels for this extraordinary ritual can be advanced. The skeletal remains provide no indication whether the mutilation occurred before or after death. Decapitation was a relatively common late Roman practice, and in some cases the head was either not placed in the grave in its correct anatomical position or was missing entirely (Philpott 1991, 77–8). Much rarer is evidence of other forms of mutilation, although Philpott (ibid., 82) lists a few examples including a decapitated burial at Dunstable, Bedfordshire, where the lower legs had been reversed and placed beside the trunk. Decapitation and other forms of mutilation are not common with Anglo-Saxon burials, although they are occasionally found (Lucy 2000, 75–8). One burial of note in the present context is a 7th-century Anglo-Saxon burial at Kemble which had both feet removed and placed by the knees (King et al. 1996, 28). Lucy (2000, 75) could find only one other example (at Loveden Hill in Lincolnshire) of this practice in Anglo-Saxon burials, and so perhaps the two examples from Gloucestershire (albeit in different cultural contexts) might be more than just coincidence. One burial at Cannington had much oak charcoal covering the skull (Rahtz et al. 2000, 369), while in the later Saxon period there was a Christian tradition of covering bodies with a layer of charcoal, perhaps in the hope of preserving the body for the Resurrection. In this practice, however, the charcoal was intimately associated with the body rather than forming the grave fill as here (ibid., 84, 418).

The arrangement of other graves in the vicinity leaves little doubt that Burial 180 was originally covered by a mound around which satellite burials clustered. The gap between burials 207 and 168, and Groups 4 and 5 to the south-east, strongly suggest the existence of a path which facilitated access to the mound for continuing ritual and reverence. The special grave at Filton invites comparison with grave 409 at Cannington which was covered by a mound into the top of which was set a box-like structure of lias slabs and a marker post or pillar (Rahtz *et al.* 2000, 57). A path led to the mound so it was evidently a continuing focus for visitation. Later burials clustered around the mound, and in some cases were dug into it. The excavators compared the grave with a series of post-Roman cist graves covered by low mounds found at sites around the western sea-board of Britain and southern Scotland including Tintagel, Cornwall and Lundy (ibid., 414; Thomas 1994, 163– 82). At Lundin Links, Fife, eight cist burials were found below a horned cairn, all certain or probable females, so it was by no means unknown for females in early medieval Britain to be chosen for prominent treatment upon death (Grieg *et al.* 2000). These special graves were probably the burial places of important people who had high-status ecclesiastical or secular associations, and sanctity was sought by burial nearby. Taken together these various traits all serve to highlight the special treatment of grave 180 at Filton, and the importance that the community attached to the burial place of this young woman.

One of the satellite graves around the central mound (Grave 248) showed evidence of having being re-opened, and was part of a sequence of intercutting burials (the only example of grave superimposition in the whole cemetery). The satellite burials around the special grave at Cannington also cut one another, a reflection of a continuing desire over time for people to be buried as close as possible to the central grave (Rahtz *et al.* 2000, 54–7). Superimposition of burials was widespread at Cannington, but Filton bears closer comparison with Ulwell, where burials were similarly arranged in ordered rows, but seven instances were found of the deliberate re-opening of graves to insert a second body within the original cut. In these cases the disarticulated bones of the primary burial were moved to one side (Cox 1988, 37–42).

The feet end of the special grave 180 was aligned 115° east of Ordnance Survey grid north (true north lies less than 1° east of grid north). This orientation was followed by the satellite burials around the mound (Group 2) and the row immediately to the south-east (Groups 4 and 5). There has been much discussion in the archaeological literature over the last few decades of the inferences that can be drawn from a study of burial orientation, much of it prompted by Rahtz's analysis at Cannington (see Rahtz *et al.* 2000, 113; Longley 2002). At Cannington the excavators concluded that in general terms the position of sunrise (or possibly sunset) had a controlling influence on the orientation of graves, although they doubted whether the solar arc model could be rigorously applied to indicate the season when burial occurred (Rahtz *et al.* 2000, 116–17). For what it is worth we may note that the south-of-east orientation adopted by the special grave at Filton compares well with the predominant orientation at Cannington.

The Filton cemetery is culturally British. South Gloucestershire and the Severn Vale remained an area under British control in the 5th and 6th centuries, to judge from the absence of Anglo-Saxon cemeteries in these areas. The nearest Anglo-Saxon cemetery to Filton is at Chavenage, 32km to the north-east, while the only cemetery in the Gloucestershire Severn Vale is at Bishop's Cleeve, in the very north of the county. Eagles (2003) has made a plausible case for the survival of a British territory which included South Gloucestershire until *c.* AD 675 when the area came within the control of the kingdom of the Hwicce, which was under Mercian dominance.

Little can be said about the religious beliefs of the people buried at Filton. The degree to which Roman Christianity survived in 5th and 6th-century western Britain, and the extent to which it was reintroduced from Ireland and Gaul, has been much debated. What is clear, however, is that the tradition of east-west aligned burials with few or no grave goods is common late Roman and post-Roman practice, and does not carry with it any necessity for the burials to be considered as Christian. Heighway (2003, 58) considers that the rulers of the western British kingdoms were nominally Christian by the early 6th century, for Gildas would surely have mentioned if they were not. South Gloucestershire had come under the jurisdiction of the Christian Hwicce by AD 679 when the bishopric based on Worcester was created. In the later 7th and early 8th centuries, minster churches were founded in some numbers within the diocese (the nearest to Filton was at Westbury-on-Trym). It is tempting to suggest that the cemetery had been abandoned by the mid 7th century due to changes that were starting to appear in the religious landscape. During the 8th century, burial in enclosed Christian graveyards, sometimes accompanied by churches, became increasingly the norm in western Britain (Petts 2002, 30), and the descendants of the people buried at Filton should presumably be sought beneath the graveyard of St Michael's church in Stoke Gifford.

Carolyn Heighway (2003, 55) has said that 'After about 600 everyone in Gloucestershire becomes invisible, at any rate to archaeologists'. The Filton cemetery is therefore a notable discovery of the physical remains of these elusive generations.

ACKNOWLEDGEMENTS

The excavations were commissioned by planning consultants Atisreal Ltd on behalf of Hewlett Packard. We would like to thank Daniel Parry-Jones, Andrew Scott and Brian McLeish of Atisreal Ltd, and Steve Hillier of Hewlett Packard, for their assistance with this project. We would also like to thank David Haigh of South Gloucestershire Council and Vanessa Straker of English Heritage for their help and encouragement, and Dr Alan Hogg, Radiocarbon Dating Laboratory, University of Waikato, for his assistance with the radiocarbon dating. The excavations were led by Kate Cullen assisted by Franco Vartuca, Sue Diamond, Andy Loader and Emily King. The fieldwork project was managed by Mark Collard, with Martin Watts managing post-excavation work. Analysis of the finds was undertaken by Ed McSloy, and of the animal bone by Sylvia Warman, who also co-ordinated the external specialist work. The illustrations were prepared by Peter Moore and initial research was undertaken by Gail Stoten (all Cotswold Archaeology). The authors are grateful to James Russell, Chris Webster, Howard Williams and Mark Collard, who all provided helpful comment on drafts of this report. The project archives and finds will be deposited with Bristol's Museums, Galleries and Archives under accession number BRSMG 2005/11.

BIBLIOGRAPHY

GRO (Gloucestershire Record Office)
    • Photocopy 258: 'A map of Stoke Gifford, the seat of John Berkeley Esq.'

Aufderheide, A.C. and Rodríguez-Martín, C. 1998 *The Cambridge encyclopedia of human palaeopathology* Cambridge, Cambridge University Press

Bayley, J. 1996 'Henley Wood: human remains' in L. Watts and P. Leach (eds) 1996, 682–720, Fiche 7–8

BGS (British Geological Survey) 1971 *1:50,000 Solid and Drift map sheet 264: Bristol*

Bonney, D. 1966 'Pagan Saxon burials and boundaries in Wiltshire', *Wiltshire Archaeol. Natur. Hist. Mag.* **61**, 25–30

Boyle, A., Jennings, D., Miles, D. and Palmer, S. 1998 *The Anglo-Saxon cemetery at Butler's Field, Lechlade, Gloucestershire. Volume 1: Prehistoric and Roman activity and Anglo-Saxon grave catalogue* Thames Valley Landscapes Monograph **10**, Oxford, Oxford Archaeological Unit

Brickley, M. and McKinley, J.I. (eds) 2004 *Guidelines to the standards for recording human remains* Institute of Field Archaeologists Paper No. **7**, Southampton/Reading, British Association of Biological Anthropology and Osteoarchaeology/Institute of Field Archaeologists

Bronk Ramsey, C. 2005 OxCal version 3.10

Brothwell, D.R. 1981 *Digging up bones* New York, Cornell University Press

CA (Cotswold Archaeology) 2003 *Hewlett Packard, Filton, South Gloucestershire and Bristol. Archaeological Desk-Based Assessment* Cotswold Archaeology unpublished report no. **03089**

CA (Cotswold Archaeology) 2005 *Hewlett Packard, Filton, South Gloucestershire and Bristol. Archaeological Evaluation* Cotswold Archaeology unpublished report no. **05031**

Caffell, A.C. 1997 *A comparison of stature between British skeletal populations and its relationship to environmental factors* University of Bradford, unpublished undergraduate dissertation

Caffell, A.C. 2004 *Dental caries in medieval Britain (c. AD 450-1540): temporal, geographical and contextual patterns* University of Durham, unpublished PhD thesis

Cox, M. 2000 'Ageing adults from the skeleton', in M. Cox and S. Mays (eds) 2000, 61–82

Cox, M. and Mays, S. (eds) 2000 *Human osteology in archaeology and forensic science* London, Greenwich Medical Media Ltd

Cox. P. 1988 'A seventh-century inhumation cemetery at Shepherd's Farm, Ulwell near Swanage, Dorset', *Proc. Dorset Natur. Hist. Archaeol. Soc.* **110**, 37–47

Eagles, B. 2003 'Augustine's Oak', *Medieval Archaeol.* **47**, 175–8

Ecclestone, M., Gardner, K., Holbrook, N. and Smith A. (eds) *The Land of the Dobunni* Oxford, Glevensis

Evison, V.I. and Hill, P. 1996 *Two Anglo-Saxon cemeteries at Beckford, Hereford and Worcester* CBA Research Report **103**, York, Council for British Archaeology

Farwell, D.E. and Molleson, T.I. 1993 *Poundbury Vol. 2: The Cemeteries* Dorchester, Dorset Natural History and Archaeology Society

Finnegan, M. 1978 'Non-metric variation of the infracranial skeleton', *J. Anatomy* **125**, 23–37

Gale, R. and Cutler, D. 2000 *Plants in Archaeology* Otley/London, Westbury Publishing/ Royal Botanic Gardens, Kew

Godman, C. 1972 'Kings Weston Hill, Bristol. Its prehistoric camps and inhumation cemetery', *Proc. Univ. Bristol Spelaeol. Soc.* **13.1**, 41–8

Grieg, C., Greig, M. and Ashmore, P. 2000 'Excavations of a cairn cemetery at lundin Links, Fife, in 1965–6', *Proc. Soc. Antiq. Scot.* **130**, 585–636

Hagen, A. 1992 *A handbook of Anglo-Saxon food: processing and consumption* Pinner, Anglo-Saxon Books

Hagen, A. 1995 *A second handbook of Anglo-Saxon food and drink: production and distribution* Hockwold-cum-Wilton, Anglo-Saxon Books

Harman, M. 1992 'Human bone from 1983', in C. Scull (ed.) 1992, 214–15

Harman, M. 1998 'The human remains', in A. Boyle *et al.* 1998, 43–52

Hearne, C. and Birbeck, V. 1999 *A35 Tolpuddle to Puddletown bypass DBFO, Dorset, 1996–8* Wessex Archaeol. Rep. **15**, Salisbury, Trust for Wessex Archaeology

Heighway, C. 2003 'Not Angels but Anglicans: the origin of the Christian church in Gloucestershire', in M. Ecclestone *et al.* 2003, 56–64

Hillson, S.W. 1996 *Dental anthropology* Cambridge, Cambridge University Press

Hirsh, L. 1983 'Cervical degenerative arthritis – possible cause of neck and arm pain', *Postgraduate Medicine* **74** (1), 123–30

Holbrook, N. 2006 'The Roman period', in N. Holbrook and J. Juřica (eds) 2006, 97–131

Holbrook, N. and Juřica, J. (eds) 2006 *Twenty-Five Years of Archaeology in Gloucestershire. A review of new discoveries and new thinking in Gloucestershire, South Gloucestershire and Bristol* Bristol and Gloucestershire Archaeol. Rep. **3**, Cirencester, Cotswold Archaeology

Holst, M. 2005 *Assessment of human bone from St Mary's primary school, Portbury, North Somerset* Osteoarchaeology Ltd unpublished report

Işcan, M.Y. and Kennedy, K.A.R. (eds) *Reconstruction of life from the skeleton* New York, Wiley-Liss

James, H. 1992 'Early medieval cemeteries in Wales', in N. Edwards and A. Lane (eds) 1992, *The Early Church in Wales and the West* Oxford, 90–103

Jancar, J. 1981 *Research at Stoke Park: mental handicap (1930-1980)* Bristol, Stoke Park Group of Hospitals – Frenchay Health District

Jones, R.H. 2006 'Bristol', in N. Holbrook and J. Juřica (eds) 2006, 189–209

King, R., Barber, A., and Timby, J. 1996 'Excavations at West Lane, Kemble: an Iron Age, Roman and Saxon burial site and a medieval building', *Trans. Bristol Gloucestershire Archaeol. Soc.* **114**, 15–54

Larsen, C.S. 1997 *Bioarchaeology: Interpreting Behaviour from the Human Skeleton* Cambridge, Cambridge University Press

Lewis, M.E. 2000 'Non-adult palaeopathology: current status and future potential', in M. Cox and S. Mays (eds) 2000, 39–57

Lewis, M.E. 2004 'Endocranial lesions in non-adult skeletons: understanding their aetiology', *Int. J. Osteoarchaeol.* **14**, 82–97

Longley, D. 2002. 'Orientation within early medieval cemeteries: some data from north-west Wales', *Antiq. J.* **82**, 309–21

Lucy, S. 2000 *The Anglo-Saxon way of death* Stroud, Sutton Publishing

Lukacs, J.R. and Rodríguez-Martín, C. 2002 'Lingual cortical mandibular defects (Stafne's Defect): an anthropological approach based on prehistoric skeletons from the Canary Islands', *Int. J. Osteoarchaeol.* **12**, 112–26

McKinley, J.I. 2004 'Compiling a skeletal inventory: disarticulated and co-mingled remains' in M. Brickley and J.I. McKinley (eds) 2004, 14–17

McKinley, J.I. and Roberts, C. 1993 *Excavation and post-excavation treatment of cremated and inhumed human remains* IFA Technical Paper **13**, Birmingham, Institute of Field Archaeologists

Marlow, C.A. 1992 'Human bone from 1989', in C. Scull (ed.) 1992, 215–20

Miles, A.E.W. 1962 'Assessment of the ages of a population of Anglo-Saxons from their dentitions', *Proc. Roy. Soc. Medicine* **55**, 881–6

Moore, W.J. and Corbett, M.E. 1971 'The distribution of dental caries in ancient British populations I. Anglo-Saxon period', *Caries Research* **5**, 151–68

Moorrees, C.F.A., Fanning, E.A. and Hunt, E.E. 1963a 'Age variation of formation stages for ten permanent teeth', *J. Dental Research* **42**, 1490–502

Moorrees, C.F.A., Fanning, E.A. and Hunt, E.E. 1963b 'Formation and resorption of three deciduous teeth in children', *American J. Physical Anthropol.* **21**, 205–13

Parker, A.J. 1978 'Stoke Gifford Roman site', *Bristol Archaeol. Res. Group Bull.* **6.6**, 152–5

Petts, D. 2002 'Cemeteries and boundaries in western Britain', in S. Lucy and A. Reynolds (eds) *Burial in Early Medieval England and Wales* (Leeds), 24–46.

Philpott, R. 1991 *Burial practices in Roman Britain* BAR British Series **219**, Oxford, British Archaeological Reports

Pritchard, J. 1911 'British archaeological notes for 1910', *Trans. Bristol Gloucestershire Archaeol. Soc.* **34**, 65–89

Rahtz, P. and Clevedon Brown, J. 1959 'Blaise Castle Hill, Bristol, 1957', *Proc. Univ. Bristol Spelaeol. Soc.* **8.3**, 147–71

Rahtz, P., Hirst, S. and Wright, S. 2000 *Cannington Cemetery* Britannia Monograph Series **17**, London, Society for the Promotion of Roman Studies

Reimer, P.J., Baillie, M.G.L., Bard, E., Bayliss, A., Beck, J.W., Bertrand, C., Blackwell, P.G., Buck, C.E., Burr, G., Cutler, K.B., Damon, P.E., Edwards, R.L., Fairbanks, R.L., Friedrich, M., Guilderson, T.P., Hughen, K.A., Kromer, B., McCormac, F.G., Manning, S., Bronk Ramsey, C., Reimer, R.W., Remmele, S., Southon, J.R., Stuiver, M., Talamo, S., Taylor, F.W., van der Plicht, J. and Weyhenmeyer, C.E. 2004 'IntCal04 Terrestrial Radiocarbon Age Calibration, 0–26 cal. kyr BP', *Radiocarbon* **46** (3), 1029–58

Roberts, C.A. and Cox, M. 2003 *Health and disease in Britain: from prehistory to the present day* Stroud, Alan Sutton

Roberts, C.A. and Manchester, K. 1995 *The archaeology of disease* (2nd Edition) Stroud, Alan Sutton

Rogers, J. 2000 'The palaeopathology of joint disease', in M. Cox and S. Mays (eds) 2000, 163–82

RPS Clouston 1992 *Bristol Business Park: Archaeological evaluation* unpublished report

Russell, J. 1989 'The archaeology of Stoke Park, Bristol', *Bristol Avon Archaeol.* **8**, 30–40

Scheuer, L. and Black, S. 2000a 'Development and ageing of the juvenile skeleton', in M. Cox and S. Mays (eds) 2000, 9–22

Scheuer, L. and Black, S. 2000b *Developmental juvenile osteology* San Diego, Academic Press

Scull, C. 1992 'Excavation and survey at Watchfield, Oxfordshire, 1983-92', *Archaeol. J.* **149**, 124–81

Stuart-Macadam, P. 1992 'Anemia in past populations', in P. Stuart-Macadam and S. Kent (eds) 1992, 151–70

Stuart-Macadam, P. and Kent, S. (eds) 1992 *Diet, demography and disease: changing perspectives of anemia* New York, Aldine de Gruyter

Stuiver, M. and Polach, H.A. 1977 'Discussion: Reporting of 14C data', *Radiocarbon* **19**, 355–63

Stuiver, M. and Reimer, P.J. 1993 'Extended 14C database and revised CALIB 3.0 14C Age calibration program', *Radiocarbon* **35** (1), 215–30

Thomas, C. 1994 *And shall the mute stones speak?* Cardiff, University of Wales Press

University of Waikato Radiocarbon Dating Laboratory 2006 'Operating Procedures', www.radiocarbondating.com (viewed on 21.04.06)

Watts, L. and Leach, P. 1996 *Henley Wood, temples and cemetery. Excavations 1962-69 by the late Earnest Greenfield and others* CBA Research Report **99**, York, Council for British Archaeology

Webster, C.J. and Brunning, R.A. 2004 'A seventh-century AD cemetery at Stoneage Barton Farm, Bishop's Lydeard, Somerset and Square-Ditched Burials in Post-Roman Britain', *Archaeol. J.* **161**, 54–81

Weddell, P. 2000 'The excavation of a post-Roman cemetery near Kenn', *Proc. Devon Archaeol. Soc.* **58**, 93–126

Wells, C. 1996 'Human burials' in V.I. Evison and P. Hill (eds) 1996, 41–62

Wessex Archaeology 1999 *Proposed Ground Modelling Area, Stoke Park* Unpublished typescript report

Williams, B. (ed.) 2004 'Review of archaeology 2001-2002', *Bristol Avon Archaeol.* **19**, 99–116

Woodward, A.B. 1993 'Part 3: Discussion', in D.E. Farwell and T.I. Molleson 1993, 215–39

Youngson, R.M. 1992 *Collins dictionary of medicine* Glasgow, Harper Collins